All You Need To Know Ab...
How To Treat It & Turr...

MINDBL...
ORGASMS
Turn Pain Into Pleasure

OLU FASOGBON

BRAND FOR SPEAKERS
BOOK PUBLISHING
Books That Transform The World

TITLE: Mindblowing Orgasms
SUBTITLE: Turn Pain Into Pleasure
All You Need To Know About Painful Intercourse, How To Treat It & Turn It Into Amazing Sex

Copyright © 2022 Olu Fasogbon | ISBN: 9798371896377

Book Design, Book Writing Coaching & Publishing done by:
Lily Patrascu
Brand for Speakers
"Books That Transform The World"
www.lily.global
www.brandforspeakers.com
+447557351222

....

https://olufasogbon.com
https://mindblowingorgasmsbook.com/
Follow me on LinkedIn: Olu Fasogbon
https://www.linkedin.com/in/olufasogbon/
Follow me on Facebook: Olu Fasogbon
https://www.facebook.com/olufasogbon/
Follow me on Instagram: @olufasogbon
https://www.instagram.com/olufasogbon/

Table Of Contents

Praise For The Book

"I loved this book because you've explained well the issues that women face daily with painful intercourse and the way you unravelled everything and provided a simple solution to make the bedroom experience wonderful. This is what most couples would love to read today to keep the fire burning for pleasure."

Dr Adaobi Onyekweli - CEO, Put You First Ltd
Bestselling Author - "Reinvent Yourself, Discover the Brilliance Within & Create Infinite Possibilities"
www.adaobionyekweli.com

"As a highly successful network marketing leader - it is great to learn about the best techniques to improve all of my life - including my sex life. This book offers some interesting tips and techniques for keeping a woman pleased and it gives me great satisfaction to be able to provide the best possible performance leveraging these amazing strategies."

Mohamed Jama, Author of "The Magnetic Leader",
Network Marketing Leader

Foreword By Lily Patrascu
Book Publisher

I met Olu Fasogbon at a health retreat event. He was a charming man with a lot of energy and enthusiasm. I was not sure at the time what he did for a living, but I did see the passion in his eyes for helping thousands of people. I could feel he had so much knowledge! So much energy; so much care and love for other people. He seemed rather timid and at the same time rather fierce in his demeanour. Like many people working in healthcare – he was always ready to provide help and assistance to other people. I loved noticing his kindness, his generous spirit, and his intelligence. I discovered much later that he was focused on helping others – especially women – overcome pain during sex and reach pleasure. Over his many years working as a pharmacist, women would come to him crying because of the then considered taboo subject – unfulfilling sex. I also realised upon further discussion with him that thousands of women suffer in silence because they are too afraid to share this with their husbands or boyfriends. I have always been passionate about empowering entrepreneurs to fulfil their dreams and that is why I decided to help Olu fulfil his dream of publishing his book, so he can help millions of couples have their desired passion and joy in their lives.

I believe being fully satisfied in every area of your personal life impacts your success at work and how joyful and fulfilled you really feel. It impacts your overall state of well-being, your excitement towards living in general and your connection with your partner. Experiencing pain or a lack of fulfilment in your love life can have a detrimental impact on everything that you do. That is why this book could turn out to be one of the most impactful books you'll ever read – especially if you are currently suffering from any of the conditions described in this book that could cause being anorgasmic or having an inability to enjoy one of the most sacred connections in the world. Grab a few copies for you and your friends to be sure you can have a fulfilling sex life, and perhaps I'll see you at one of the worldwide speaking tours Olu will deliver around this topic.

Lily Patrascu
Book Publisher
www.lily.global

About The Book

Are you experiencing undesirable pain during sexual intercourse? Are you alone and in tears, unable to talk to anyone? Are you looking for a cure? Have you had a great sex life that turned into a nightmare and ended completely when menopause started? Do you want to do away with anxiety, fear, and depression due to this problem? This book will give you guidance and information on how you can handle pain during intercourse with your partner and experience Multiple Mindblowing Orgasms following various orgasm systems I've designed so you can share a pleasurable moment together.

Mindblowing sex can have an astounding effect on your well-being and the connection you have with your partner. It can strengthen the love that united you and your partner in the first place. Lack of great sex can have the opposite effect. Thousands of women every year experience painful sex and are having to cope with feelings of inadequacy, shame, guilt, and a sense of not being good enough. Whether you have always experienced painful sex or you have started experiencing it recently, there is hope for you.

In this book, you will discover how both of you can enjoy the moment smoothly. You will learn and cultivate ideas for managing your sex life. You will discover techniques to keep you energetic and alive. This book will unleash your understanding of handling the unexplainable pain that you experienced in the past. It will give you the tools to live happily and keep you excited in your day-to-day life. You will find out how to live the same way as others enjoying their sex life and to have delight every second with your partner.

The ideas and information that you will read in this book will not only help you in your sex life, but will also impact your everyday life. You will unlock ways in which you can be more passionate every day. You will find out how you can leverage your newly found sexual energy to be very productive at work. This book will reveal the secrets of how you can achieve mindblowing orgasms over and over again.

About The Author

Olu Fasogbon is a passionate pharmacist and sexual health coach with over forty years of experience helping people with their health and well-being concerns. After seeing many women crying in his pharmacy over the issue of painful sex and lack of orgasm, Olu spent many years researching, mastering the topic, and discovering the very best solutions.

Olu is the creator of Multiple Mindblowing Orgasms systems that can contribute towards having an incredible sexual experience. The author's varied roles working in hospitals and community practice in the UK, whilst interacting with patients at different levels, gave him an in-depth understanding of health and well-being. Olu offers supported care and accommodation for patients with disabilities.

He is a heart-centred mentor and entrepreneur, having supported people at various levels to achieve their goals and being part of philanthropic ventures in the UK and in Nigeria, where he sponsors the education of many and looks after the well-being of needy people with monthly financial support. As the chairman of the board of trustees in a couple of churches, he has been supporting missionary activities around the world. He is a devout Christian, a pharmacist, and married to Folashade Fasogbon, a chartered accountant.

Note To The Reader

Are you unhappy at the mere thought or mention of the words 'sex' and 'intercourse'? Are you worried sick that your husband will try again tonight and leave you in agony from the pain that you go through every time this happens? Are you afraid of refusing him again tonight on account of the pain because no matter how gentle he tries to be, it is still painful? Are you holding back your tears so that he doesn't know that you are suffering? Or are you blaming yourself for all this? Or are you blaming him? If the answer is yes to at least one of the above questions, we both know why. A lot of women today are living their life in this agony, day in, day out, night in, night out. It is not a subject that most women are comfortable discussing even with their spouses, let alone with third parties. Many have ended up with depression, work problems, and sometimes even broken marriages because of painful sex.

If you too are struggling with the questions we discussed here, I have good news for you! You can change this situation and transform your sex life if you follow the simple step-by-step recommendations mentioned in this book. You are definitely not alone. Many women do not experience orgasms in their lifetime because they do not have access to the right information and guidance. Women deserve to reach climax as men do. Also, even if you have experienced orgasms, you may have heard that there is a greater dimension called multiple orgasms. If so, there is one step you need to take and that is to learn what multiple orgasms mean – and then, learn what you need to do to enjoy them. Are you dreaming that one day you too will experience the peak of sexual joy? If yes, you are in the right place to learn and achieve your dream.

Put this book close to your red nightie and dream on, because you are about to get on a roller coaster ride. Try some of the techniques stated in the book and let me know how it is. Tonight could be the night that you become the NEW WOMAN, who is sexually fulfilled and full of joy!!!

My Story

Many years ago, I was a young, vibrant, energetic and fresh pharmacist working in a pharmacy in the United Kingdom. A voluptuous, gorgeous-looking woman came in to see me. I could see that she was troubled. 'How can I help?' I asked. The tears started rolling. I was almost embarrassed. I waited for her to calm down as she tried to compose herself. As soon as she started speaking the tears came flowing again.

I tried to reassure her and told her that whatever her problem was I would do my best to help her. She said that having sex was her biggest nightmare because it was painful every time. She had been married for a few years and had two children, but the problem persisted. She tried most of the time to hide it from her husband in order not to make him feel bad or distressed. She, however, tried to reduce their intimacy to the minimum.

I asked her a few personal questions and realised that she was not comfortable discussing the subject. I realised that there was not a one-consultation solution that would solve her problem. I put it out of my mind, thinking it was an isolated incident. A friend of mine asked his friend, Mr A, to have a chat with me about something that was bothering him on the off chance that I might put him on the right track for a solution.

Mr A had been married for over a year to a beautiful, voluptuous wife. Both families spent a great deal of money on the wedding, a massive affair in India. Mr A told me that he had made up his mind on what to do but he just wanted to see if I could suggest something to help him. He said that he had succeeded in having penetration with his wife only twice in the fifteen months of their marriage.

Every time he tried to have sex with his wife, she would get annoyed and say marriage is not all about sex. 'So what have you decided to do?' I asked. He said that he had decided to return her to her parents and then initiate divorce proceedings. Mr A and his wife were well-educated professionals. I asked him to bring his wife for a chat. He told me that she would not come as he had tried to get her to see the GP and she refused.

She could not see herself discussing such a matter with an unknown person. I began to realise that this problem was more common than I thought. Nobody should ever have to suffer like she did – EVERY night. I didn't know it at the time, but millions of women worldwide suffer from painful sex. I had empathy for her and as a pharmacist who deeply cared about helping others, I could feel her deep pain.

All of a sudden, I started seeing people very close to me going through this experience and suffering in silence. There were several such cases that helped me find my purpose. I made it my mission to help women overcome their sex-related issues, including the myths they shared, so that discussing them was no longer taboo.

I wanted to help them understand that sex or orgasms are all normal physiological functions of the body, just like breathing and heartbeats, and that it was absolutely fine to have issues with sex as they could be treated and managed in just the way we manage our other health issues. I decided to start by writing a book that could reach every nook and corner of the world, a book women and even men will read to understand what sex, orgasms, and painful sex are all about.

This book is intended to be a one-stop guide for all women who are struggling in silence with painful intercourse. Coming back to the couple from India, her husband finally managed to arrange our meeting. I used this opportunity to make her feel at ease and helped her with some information that helped her understand that sex is an important part of marriage. It took her some time to realise the benefits of sex for a happy marriage and even for their overall health.

And this set the ball rolling towards the realisation that paved the way for the couple to mark a new beginning in their married life and, of course, their sex life. But THIS was definitely not the end! It was, in fact, a new beginning ... a new purpose. Why should women continue to suffer due to painful intercourse? I started working on my mission and here I am today presenting you this book to provide you with all that you need to know about sex, painful sex, getting orgasms, and even super orgasms!

Chapter 1
Get In The Mood To Be Sexually Rejuvenated

Painful sex is silently experienced by millions of women worldwide. You are not alone. Why do women prefer to bear it silently rather than discuss it with someone? Painful sex is something that many women experience once or several times due to different causes. Yet, it is very rarely discussed. Not everyone suffering painful sex consults their doctor, perhaps because women feel embarrassed about the issue. This is why some women bear it silently even if WONDERFUL TREATMENTS are available to have it relieved completely.

Why Does Painful Sex Exist?

Although painful sex affects men as well, it is more common in women. The pain is felt in the genital area or in the pelvis. In some cases, women may experience pain before, during, and after sex. To understand painful sex clearly, let me share some information about the anatomy or the physical structure of a woman's genital area.

Women's Sexual Anatomy

The sexual anatomy of a woman's body includes the vulva, and the internal reproductive organs, such as the uterus and ovaries. We will focus more on the external parts that play an active role in sexual activities. The vulva is the part of the female genitalia that is on the outside of the body. It consists of the vaginal opening, labia, clitoris, and the external urethral opening through which we pass urine.

Though the vagina is just a part of the vulva, when most people say 'vagina', they actually mean the vulva. But the vulva has a lot going on within it especially when it comes to sexual intercourse. Any abnormality, including the slightest injury or infection in this region, could be a reason why you experience so much pain during intercourse. This marks the importance of why you need to know your vulva better to avoid painful sex. Moving forward, let's learn about the parts of the vulva, starting from the outermost, the labia. The labia is like the lips of the vagina. These are the folds of skin around the vaginal opening.

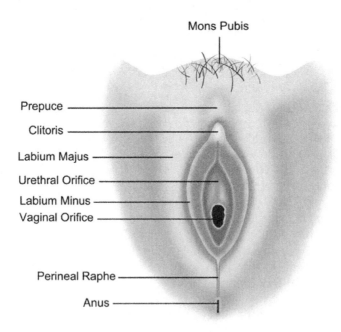

The outer folds, called the labia majora, are usually more fleshy and thicker, and protected by pubic hair. The labia minora, also called the inner lips, are along the inner side of the outer lips. The labia, being the outermost part of the genitals, are more likely to get bruises, injuries, or even infections that spread from the skin surrounding the genital area.

This is why it is important to maintain optimum hygiene of the external genitals to prevent painful sex. The clitoris is located at the upper tip of the vulva, where both the inner lips meet. The vaginal and urethral openings are located slightly deeper between the two inner lips. The vaginal opening is present below the urethral opening.

The vaginal opening extends deeper to meet the cervix which, in turn, extends to the uterus. The vaginal tube connects your vulva to the cervix and is lined by a delicate layer of mucosa. The vaginal walls also have a layer of muscles that tend to contract and relax during sexual activities as well as childbirth. The vaginal opening is where menstrual blood flows out and babies leave the body. It is also where the penis is inserted during sexual intercourse, and where you insert menstrual cups or tampons.

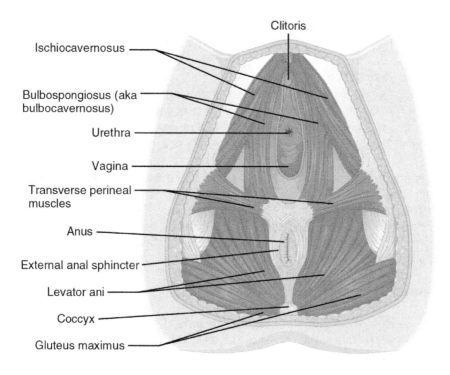

Take a look at the picture above to get a better understanding of your vaginal structure. The health and hygiene of your vagina, vaginal canal, and the mucosa and muscles lining it can play a huge role in the development of pain during sex.

We will discuss this later when we talk about the causes of painful sex. The other parts of the vulva include the anus and the mons. Deeper into the vagina lie the other sexual and reproductive organs, including the cervix, uterus, fallopian tubes, and ovaries. These structures do not take an active part in sexual activities and hence are not directly linked to the causes of painful sex.

The Manifestation Of Painful Sex

Most women suffering from painful sex experience pain during intercourse, while some may experience pain before and after sexual activities.

Here are some common indications for painful sex:
- Persistent pain in the vulva or vagina.
- Pain during penetration.
- Pain at the onset of or after penetration. The pain may persist even while wearing a tampon.
- Itching in the vulva or vagina.
- Pain in the inner part of the genitals, felt during deeper thrusts.
- A burning sensation in the vagina or vulva before, during, and after intercourse, or while passing urine.
- Throbbing pain, which continues for several hours after sex.

It is important to realise that the pain caused by sex is like any other pain that occurs due to conditions such as arthritis or muscle stiffness. Instead of ignoring it or accepting it, you should take steps to understand the issue and look for solutions. I hope that knowing the signs and symptoms of pain during sex opens the door for you to seek appropriate treatment as soon as possible.

Causes Of Painful Sex

The causes of painful sex can be categorised into physical factors or emotional factors. The physical factors can be further categorised depending on whether the pain occurs at the time of penetration or during deep thrusting.

Let's check it out:

Bridling Entry Pain

Entry pain that occurs at the time of penetration could be associated with several factors, including the following.

Lack Of Lubrication

This is a common cause of painful sex in older or menopausal women, as well as in young women. Lack of lubrication may occur due to fluctuations in hormonal levels during and after menopause. A drop in the production of a female sex hormone called oestrogen after childbirth and during breastfeeding can also make the vagina dry, causing painful sex.

In younger women, it could be the result of not having enough foreplay. Foreplay is essential before the actual penetration of the penis into the vagina. Adequate foreplay can arouse a woman and stimulate the secretion of mucus in the vagina. The mucus can enhance the lubrication of the vaginal canal thus facilitating the smooth entry of the penis. Lack of foreplay can prevent arousal and lubrication, thus increasing the chances of having painful intercourse.

Medication

Some medications are known to affect women's sexual arousal and decrease lubrication, making intercourse painful. Some of these include birth control pills, sedatives, antidepressants, antihypertensives, and antihistamines, which are used to treat allergies.

Unforeseen Accidents

Injury, irritation, or trauma due to pelvic surgery or accidents can lead to pain and swelling in the genital region and increase the risk of pain during sex. Women may also experience painful intercourse after they have had an episiotomy, which is a cut made in the vulva or vagina during delivery to enlarge the vaginal canal to facilitate childbirth.

However, painful intercourse caused due to these factors is often temporary and tends to disappear once the injury or surgical wound is healed.

Inflammation And Infection

An infection in the genital area or even urinary tract may cause painful intercourse. Fungal, viral, or bacterial infections of the skin surrounding the vulva, or other skin problems such as eczema affecting the genital area, can also cause irritation, inflammation and ulceration of the tissues, resulting in pain during intercourse.

Contraction of Muscles

Vaginismus refers to involuntary spasms of the muscles in the walls of the vaginal canal. The spasm of these muscles may occur due to stress or fear, making penetration painful.

Congenital Abnormalities

Some women may experience painful sex due to a congenital anomaly present at birth, like vaginal agenesis or imperforate hymen.

Vaginal agenesis refers to the absence of a completely formed vagina, while imperforate hymen refers to the presence of a membrane blocking the vaginal opening. Surgical intervention to correct these abnormalities could provide considerable relief from painful sex.

Taming Deep Pain

Painful intercourse may be due to deep pain that occurs during and after a deep thrust. The causes of deep pain are different from the causes of entry pain. Deep pain, just as the name suggests, usually occurs due to issues related to the organs deep within the vaginal canal. It often becomes worse in certain positions.

The common causes of deep pain include the following.

Pre-existing Illnesses

Pre-existing medical conditions affecting the uterus, ovaries, bowels, and bladder may cause painful intercourse. Some of these conditions include endometriosis, uterine prolapse, pelvic inflammatory disease, pelvic floor dysfunction, cystitis, uterine fibroids, retroverted uterus, irritable bowel syndrome, adenomyosis, ovarian cysts, and haemorrhoids.

Medical Treatments And Surgeries

Internal scarring due to pelvic surgery, such as hysterectomy, may cause pain during intercourse. Treatment for cancer, like chemotherapy and radiation, may also be responsible for making intercourse painful.

Emotional Causes

Sexual intercourse is linked with intense emotions such as pleasure and satisfaction. However, in some women, emotional factors may contribute to painful intercourse.

Emotional factors responsible for painful sex include:

Psychological Symptoms

Women who suffer from anxiety and depression are more likely to experience painful sex. Women who are concerned about their physical appearance or have a fear of intimacy may have low sexual arousal, resulting in pain and discomfort during intercourse.

Conquer Stress

Mental stress and anxiety may cause tightening of all the muscles in the body, including the muscles in the vaginal wall and the pelvic floor, resulting in painful intercourse.

Emotional Trauma Or Sexual Abuse

Women who have had emotional trauma during childhood or early adulthood may suffer from pain during sex. Failed personal relationships, being cheated on by an earlier partner, and a history of physical or sexual abuse can prevent sexual arousal and cause painful sex.

Attitude Towards Sex

Fear, guilt, and shame related to sex can also prevent women from enjoying sexual activities and prevent arousal, thus causing dryness and pain during sex.

What's Next?

Painful sex can be treated! You can now start assessing why you are suffering from this problem. Once you recognise the possible causes, whether single or multiple, it will be much easier for you to take appropriate steps to avoid pain, enjoy sexual intercourse and even achieve orgasm!

Chapter 2
A Roadblock To Your Sexual Adventure

Many women prefer to avoid any medical treatment for painful intercourse. They consider it an issue that is too embarrassing to discuss with a doctor. Also, most women believe that it's only a simple problem that can be ignored. They do not think that it is important enough to be treated or are simply unaware of the complications that can arise due to improper diagnosis and treatment.

As a result, the issue persists and leads to several other problems that can affect not just the sexual life of the couple, but also the physical and mental health of the affected woman. Needless to say, ignoring painful intercourse may also lead to strained relations between the woman and her spouse and create difficulties in her personal life.

Poor Mental Health

It is not unknown for women to develop mental health issues that can be traced back to painful intercourse. They may experience severe mental stress and anxiety, especially before and during intercourse. This can have serious short-term and long-term effects on their emotional health.

Women experiencing painful sex are more likely to develop psychological disorders like depression. They may also experience abnormal behaviours in terms of their personal and social interactions. They may avoid visiting relatives and friends, or attending any events due to the desire to stay aloof from anyone who might ask them about their personal life.

Over a period of time, they may also develop more serious problems that can be avoided by treating this condition in a timely manner. Early diagnosis and making an effort to find why it exists could help women avoid stress and anxiety and improve their mental health.

Strained Personal Relations

The first negative impact of painful sex is noticed in the personal relations of the couple. When the female partner experiences pain during intercourse, she might try to avoid close contact with her spouse and avoid intimacy. She may resist any cues by the spouse for sexual intercourse. She would rather maintain some distance in order to avoid any sexual intimacy. This can create a rift between the couple and strain their relations.

Painful sex experienced by a woman may also have an impact on the emotional health of her spouse as he might feel deprived of sexual pleasure and thus experience a lack of satisfaction and sexual fulfilment in life. Fortunately, in some cases, men do care for the feelings and emotions of their partner and avoid any intimacy that could create anxiety in her mind. They often encourage their partner to find the causes of pain in intercourse.

However, even in such cases, the lack of sexual satisfaction might have an adverse impact on the personal relationship of the couple, resulting in frequent conflicts, disagreements, and misunderstandings.

The strain in personal relations can be easily avoided by having an open discussion with each other. Women should be open with their partners about the pain and anxiety they feel during intercourse. They can also talk about their expectations from each other so that conflict related to the lack of sexual satisfaction can be avoided.

Misdiagnosis

Many women avoid seeking treatment for painful sex. Some resort to self diagnosis which puts them at risk of misdiagnosis due to lack of adequate knowledge on the subject. Also there are others who are shy of the subject and avoid their physician or misrepresent their symptoms and do not get the correct treatment due to the incorrect representation and interpretation of their symptoms.

For example, it has been observed that women who suffer from vaginismus may be overly anxious before and during intercourse. They may even have panic attacks. These symptoms are often not limited just to sexual relations. The fear of having sex may linger in their mind throughout the day and affect their emotional health as well as actions and behaviours. They even get angry at trifles or behave in an irritated manner for no apparent reason.

There is a risk of these symptoms being diagnosed as mental health issues. In some cases, the patient may be advised to seek the help of a physician or a psychiatrist to address anxiety, depression, or panic attacks instead of taking care of the primary cause, which is vaginismus.

If the real cause of anxiety and depression is not revealed during the consultation with the psychiatrist, the woman may just end up taking medication like antidepressants that would only relieve her emotional symptoms to some extent while also causing serious side effects.

At the same time, it will do nothing to address the primary issue, which will persist. And as long as the vaginismus or other cause of painful sex is not eliminated, the patient will continue to have anxiety and panic attacks in spite of taking antidepressants.

These problems are linked to avoiding treatment for painful sex. Ignoring or feeling too shy to discuss the symptoms of painful intercourse may lead to the misdiagnosis of the condition. It can increase the chances of receiving incorrect treatment and further worsen the problems. This is why it is really important to correctly diagnose and treat painful sex.

Delayed Treatment

Oftentimes, because of misdiagnosis, painful sex is likely to lead to serious complications due to the delayed treatment of the underlying cause. In some women, the cause of painful sex could be as simple as vaginal or cervical infections. The use of appropriate antibiotics, antiviral, or antifungal drugs can help to clear the infection and enable women to have intercourse without any pain or discomfort.

In some women, painful intercourse can occur due to the dryness of the vagina linked to hormonal changes occurring after pregnancy and menopause. It can also be due to the side effects of birth control pills or other medications they are using.

This can be treated easily by avoiding the use of these drugs, or undergoing hormone replacement therapy, or by simply using lubricants to allow smooth entry of the penis.

However, not taking treatment for painful sex can allow these underlying diseases to persist and progress. The infection in the vagina or cervix may become worse, causing damage to the tissues or spreading to other organs. The side effects of medications can result in more serious complications. This marks the need to seek early medical intervention in order to avoid the delay in treatment and prevent complications.

Infertility

When painful sex is an issue, the couple is likely to refrain from any intimate sexual relationship due to which conception, very obviously, fails to occur. In fact, the inability to get pregnant is a common reason why most couples visit a doctor. And it is during this consultation that painful sex is revealed to be the cause of the problem.

It is surprising to know that women would rather avoid discussing their sexual problems with anyone, but at the same time are eager to undergo intensive treatments like IUI and IVF when it comes to their desire to conceive.

Luckily the perspectives are changing. While not all of today's women are reluctant to discuss their sexual problems, we still have a long way to go before we are able to address this issue with the same ease we talk about joint pains, diabetes, or hypertension.

Lack Of Work Productivity

Your job performance might take a hit when you are reeling under the stress of painful intercourse and strained personal relations. You may not be able to focus on your projects and activities at the workplace when, at the back of your mind, you are worried about your sexual difficulties.

This is just another reason why women should never ignore painful sex and should ensure that they receive proper treatment so that they can excel in all spheres of life including their personal relations, emotional health, social interactions, job performance, motherhood, and lastly but most importantly, sexual pleasure and orgasms.

Conclusion

Pain during sex may cause issues in the couple's sexual relationship. It may also produce a negative effect on their personal life, in addition to causing emotional conflicts and physical pain.

There are several effective treatments available for women to overcome pain during intercourse. Instead of ignoring this condition, they should seek appropriate treatment in order to avoid its impact on their personal life, and emotional and physical health.

Proper diagnosis and treatment of painful sex would help women enjoy sex and enable them to have a healthy and happy personal life. Continue reading to know more about diagnosing painful sex so that the exact cause of painful intercourse can be identified. Proper diagnosis of the underlying causes is the key to receiving the best treatment.

Chapter 3
Discover The Roots Of Your Agony

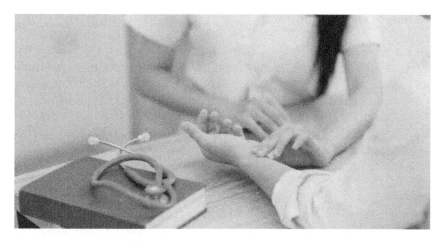

The medical evaluation for painful intercourse usually consists of a complete physical examination, and laboratory and imaging tests to detect the possible causes. It should be noted that painful intercourse can occur due to one or multiple causes. Hence, the complete medical history of the patient and physical examination and tests are necessary to identify all the possible factors that could be contributing to pain during intercourse.

Let's take a quick look at the diagnostic methods aimed at identifying the underlying causes of painful sex.

Medical History

Medical history regarding when the pain began, and when and where it hurts, could provide valuable clues to the diagnosis of painful sex. Women who suffer from painful sex due to fear and anxiety may find it difficult to tell the exact location of pain, while those with infections would be able to tell where exactly it hurts the most. The physician may also ask the patient to describe the type of pain and whether it occurs during all sexual positions and with every sexual partner. Your doctor may also ask questions related to surgical history, sexual history, and childbirth, to assess the possible causes. The history of having an episiotomy or any operative procedure recently could indicate these factors to be the possible causes and the pain being temporary in nature. Please do not let embarrassment and shyness stop you from answering these questions truthfully. The answers to these questions can help the physician know the exact cause of your pain and suggest appropriate treatment.

A Pelvic Examination

During a pelvic examination, the physician can check the tissues for signs of infection, irritation, or anatomical problems. The doctor may also try to locate the pain by gently applying mild pressure to the pelvic muscles and genitals. A visual examination of the vagina with the help of an instrument called a speculum can also be performed to check for signs of infection or trauma. The spasm of the muscles during examination could help in the diagnosis of vaginismus as a factor responsible for pain during sex.

Other Tests

Depending on your physical examination and medical and sexual history, you may need to undergo further tests to confirm the diagnosis.

These tests may include:
- Complete blood count to detect changes in the levels of white cells that could confirm the diagnosis of infection
- Vaginal swab to detect infection
- Blood tests for the diagnosis of sexually transmitted infections such as herpes, HIV, syphilis, gonorrhoea, and hepatitis C
- Ultrasound examination of the pelvis and abdomen to detect abnormalities of the uterus, ovaries, bladder, and bowels
- Hormonal tests to detect abnormalities in the production of oestrogen and progesterone

Early diagnosis of the primary and secondary causes of painful sex could help women to take appropriate steps to correct abnormalities. It would help them eliminate the factors responsible for causing pain during intercourse and allow them to enjoy sex without any difficulties and with higher intimacy and pleasure and plenty of orgasms.

Chapter 4
Home Remedies: Road to Orgasm

Millions of women suffer from pain during sex and it has been my mission to help them overcome it. That is why I have created the Pain Free System – which gives an overview of the steps required to start the journey to having amazing sex.

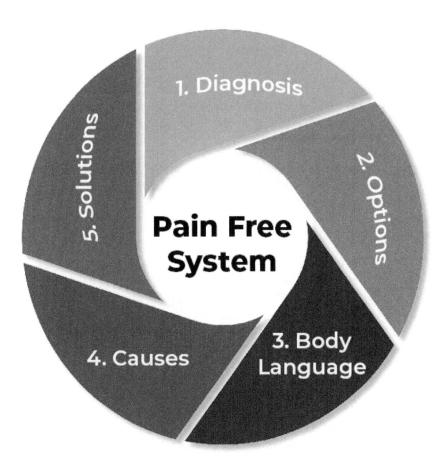

The Pain Free System is a shortcut to the key actions you need to take to fast-track your results. The system will serve as a quick guide to the key action points and things that you need to do regularly to sustain your results and live a sexually fulfilling life.

Pain Free System

1. Diagnosis

The first step of the system is to have an effective diagnosis. Diagnosis is crucial as it determines the right treatment that would provide the desired results. We must also get the diagnosis right so that the treatment helps to eliminate the root cause and the results are long-lasting.

2. Options

The second step is to consider all the options available to tackle the facts, symptoms, and underlying conditions related to the diagnosis.

3. Body Knowledge

Your body knowledge is the third step. You know your body better than anyone else. Your body knowledge, therefore, comes into play. You can determine what suits you best in all the options that will be made available to you. You have the choice to try others if one fails until you get the right fit.

4. Causes

What caused this problem? Sometimes, knowing the cause itself could be the diagnosis of the problem. Were you sexually abused as a child? You may have to think deeply in order to discover where things started going wrong. This is important to ensure you are able to identify the root cause and follow the treatments that can yield the best results.

5. Solutions

The fifth step is the solution. This would come from steps one to four. Taking action is the crucial point in step five. If you get everything else right and know exactly what to do but you fail to take action the whole purpose is defeated.

Powerful Home Remedies For Your Distress

Panic is what most women do when they suffer from painful intercourse. They avoid their spouse. This is very common. And they don't avoid their partner just during sex, but at all times, to avoid any intimacy. As discussed earlier, this can have a huge negative impact on your personal relations. Instead of getting panicked or feeling anxious or avoiding your spouse, you can try some simple home remedies that will take away the pain from intercourse and bring pleasure.

Several medications and products are specifically recommended for women who suffer from painful intercourse. Most of these medications are highly effective. But these medications have specific uses, which means each medicine is suitable only to manage one or more specific causes of painful sex. Hence, you will need to consult your gynaecologist before you start using them. If you are not in favour of using medications or are still feeling too shy to discuss your problems with a gynaecologist, you may first try some simple home remedies to stop painful intercourse.

Let us look at some of the most effective home remedies that would help you prevent pain during intercourse and help you enjoy sexual pleasure.

The Pain Free System gives an overview of the key actions you need to take to get immediate or near-instant solutions to your symptoms. Subsequently, this system will serve as a quick guide to the key action points and things that you can do daily to give you that amazing sex life.

The solutions are divided into solutions for pain caused by penetration and pain caused by emotional factors.

Pain Free Solutions System: Pain From Penetration

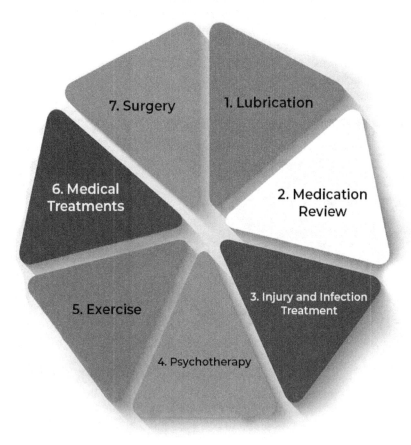

Pain Free Solutions System

Pain From Penetration:

- **Lubrication**
  The use of lubrication during intercourse would help avoid pain caused due to friction and enhance the sense of pleasure.

- **Medication Review**
  Check the medications you are using regularly and ask your doctor if any of those could be interfering with your hormonal balance or sexual and reproductive functions.

- **Injury and Infection Treatment:**
  If you have any injuries or sores on your genitals, seek immediate treatment. Ask your doctor if you need to refrain from sexual activity until the infection or injury has healed completely. This is essential to protect yourself and your partner against sexually transmitted infections.

- **Psychotherapy**
  Consult a psychiatrist if your sexual problem can be traced to mental stress, anxiety, or fear, due to factors like childhood abuse, trauma, or any other reason.

- **Exercise**
  Perform regular exercises like simple walking and swimming to improve mood, enhance stamina, and restore hormonal balance. Consider Kegel exercises to strengthen the pelvic floor muscles.

- **Medical Treatments**
  Medical treatments like hormonal preparations may be needed if the cause is linked to an underlying disorder such as pelvic inflammatory disease, endometriosis, uterine fibroids, or any disorder that causes hormonal imbalance.

- **Surgery**
  Surgery may be needed should the results of tests like ultrasonography of your lower abdomen reveal a structural abnormality.

Pain Free Solutions System: Emotional Causes Of Pain

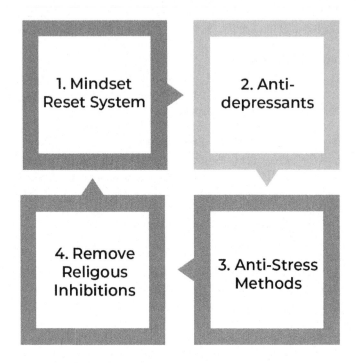

Emotional Causes Of Pain:

1. **Mindset Reset System**
   You can try the 'Mindset Reset System' or 'Image Booster Therapy' to change your attitude toward yourself and your spouse, as well as the world in general. It would help boost your self-esteem and self-confidence, and reduce fear and anxiety, thus allowing you to develop a positive and more exciting perspective on sex.

2. **Antidepressants**
   If you are diagnosed with severe depression or anxiety disorders, you might need to use antidepressants. It is best to consult a psychiatrist who would prescribe the most suitable antidepressant for you and also suggest other therapies to relieve stress and anxiety.

3. **Anti-Stress Methods**

   Try natural anti-stress methods like yoga, meditation, and aromatherapy to overcome stress, which is a major cause as well as the effect of painful sex.

4. **Remove Religious Inhibitions**

   If your religious beliefs or inhibitions are preventing you from enjoying sex, you may seek the help of your spiritual leader(s) to get deeper insights into the issues.

Communication With Partner

There is no better way to avoid painful sex than talking to your partner. Most couples are able to find good solutions to their problem simply by discussing it with each other. This can be the first step you can take to help yourself and your partner to enjoy sex. You can discuss with your partner what feels good, including foreplay or any specific position, and what doesn't. You may also ask your partner to go slow or avoid deep penetration if that hurts. Talking to your partner will allow him to understand why you feel so anxious or why you are avoiding him and help him take appropriate steps to alleviate your anxiety and fears. Also, until vaginal sex becomes less painful, you and your spouse may try other ways to get intimate.

Kissing, sensual massage, and mutual masturbation offer perfect alternatives to sexual intercourse. It may even be more comfortable, more fun, and more fulfilling than your regular routine.

Change In Positions

You will be surprised to know that just a simple change in your sexual position could help you avoid painful intercourse. Some women experience pain during sex due to anatomical abnormalities of the cervix, vagina, or uterus. In such cases, slightly changing your position during sex can mean the specific part where it hurts the most can be left undisturbed during the activity.

This may seem to be too simple. However, a large number of women have experienced significant relief from pain by following this method. A change in position may also be helpful for women who suffer from painful sex due to vaginal or cervical infections. Hence, if you have sharp or severe pain during deep penetration, you can try different positions, like being on top.

This position would reduce pressure or thrust on the parts that hurt. It can also allow you to regulate penetration only to a depth that feels comfortable to you and thus prevent the pain.

Don't Rush

Most gynaecologists advise couples to avoid rushing into sex. This advice is useful for patients who suffer from painful intercourse and men who suffer from sexual difficulties like erectile dysfunction and premature ejaculation, or even couples who have infertility issues.

Gynaecologists often recommend having good foreplay before the intercourse instead of rushing.

Longer foreplay would help to stimulate the natural lubrication in your vagina and prevent dryness, which is a major cause of pain during penetration. Having longer foreplay will also allow you to feel fully aroused and thus reduce your anxiety. During foreplay, it may also help to communicate with each other to share how you are feeling. It's best to let your partner know what you like or guide him to do what feels good. Longer foreplay may help women avoid pain during intercourse and substantially increase their sexual satisfaction.

Use Lubricants

Dryness of the vagina is one of the most common causes of painful sex. The vagina is lined by a mucus membrane that secretes sticky discharge, which allows smooth entry of the penis during sex. Dryness of the vagina prevents enough lubrication due to which you may experience friction or rubbing of the penis against the vaginal mucosa, causing pain.

When this happens recurrently, it may damage the delicate vaginal tissues resulting in tears, injuries, and bruises that can worsen the pain further. Hence, it is essential to address vaginal dryness to prevent pain during sex. If the natural vaginal lubrication does not seem to be adequate, you may use artificial lubricants to allow smooth and seamless penetration.

A personal lubricant would make intercourse more comfortable. There are several different brands of lubricants specifically meant to be used during sex, and most of them are safe and effective. You may try a few brands to choose the one that suits you the best. You can apply the lubricant to your vagina or your partner's penis right before sex.

If you are not in menopause or use condoms during sex, you can try using water-based lubricants. Remember that oil-based lubricants may damage condoms, making them less effective.

Empty Your Bladder

Having a full bladder during sex could be one of the causes of pain. Most women drink herbal teas, milk, or other beverages before or after dinner or just before bedtime. As a result, the bladder becomes full and presses against the uterus and cervix. During sex, when the partner exerts pressure on these parts, women may experience pain and discomfort.

The pain may become worse during penetration, especially when the couple tries common sexual positions like 'man on top'. In this position, the entire weight of the man's body is exerted on the bladder, causing pain. Hence, women who suffer from pain during intercourse should try emptying their bladder before sex.

They should also limit their intake of fluids after dinner and before bedtime and see if it works.

Take A Warm Bath

A warm bath can provide several benefits that could help you avoid painful intercourse. Having a warm bath or shower could ease mental stress and help you avoid anxiety during sex. A warm bath may also relax the muscles in your body. This can help relieve body aches and even prevent spasms of the vaginal muscles during sex.

A warm bath is often good for stimulating your sexual senses and causing arousal, making you more receptive to sexual intercourse. These benefits of a warm bath could be beneficial for women who suffer from painful sex due to tiredness, body aches, stress, or vaginal spasms.

Apply An Ice Pack

Applying an ice pack to the vulva is one of the most effective home remedies for managing painful sex. If you have sharp pain in the external parts of the genitals, such as the vulva, you can try applying ice packs before and after sex. This can work in several ways to ease the pain. Ice packs could be beneficial for relieving muscle spasms thereby preventing pain during intercourse. It may also help to reduce swelling and redness in the vulva and vagina caused by infections. This simple home remedy may also ease pain due to minor injuries or bruises and help you enjoy sex.

If you are suffering from pain during intercourse, you can start with these home remedies. It is likely that you will find significant relief from your symptoms. You may try medications or other advanced treatments when these home remedies do not provide any relief. But, most women actually don't need any active medical intervention when they simply change their sexual position or try other home remedies we have discussed here.

Chapter 5
Get The Best Pleasure Ever Experienced

Let's take a look at the medical interventions that would help you avoid painful intercourse.

Medications For Painful Sex:

Hormonal Preparations

Hormonal changes are common causes of painful sex in menopausal, pregnant, and breastfeeding women. Dwindling levels of oestrogen and other hormonal shifts can make the tissues in the vagina dry and thin. That dryness, in turn, can cause friction during penetration, resulting in pain.

Also, as women age, the muscles and other tissues in the vagina can lose their elasticity. This may occur due to the reduced production of two major components of the skin matrix – elastin and collagen – due to ageing, as well as a decline in levels of oestrogen. The reduced levels of these components prevent adequate stretching of the vagina due to which it may feel tight.

This is another common cause of painful sex that can be managed by using hormonal preparations to improve estrogen levels. The use of topical oestrogen creams directly applied to the vagina may help to stimulate the secretion of natural lubricants. It may also enhance the production of elastin and collagen in the vaginal tissues and thus, provide relief from the symptoms of painful sex.

Oestrogen may also improve the flexibility and thickness of the vaginal tissues and enhance blood flow. Topical oestrogen is available in the form of creams, tablets, flexible rings, and inserts. The vaginal cream needs to be applied to the vulva and inside of the vagina about two to three times per week.

The vaginal tablet is to be inserted into the vagina two times a week with your fingers or using an applicator. The vaginal ring also needs to be inserted into the vagina, where it stays for up to three months. In the UK, NICE (the National Institute for Health and Care Excellence) and in the US, the FDA (Food and Drug Administration), have approved a medication, ospemifene, to manage moderate to severe cases of painful sex due to the lack of adequate vaginal lubrication.

This medication works by acting like oestrogen to reduce the declining impact in the production of this hormone due to ageing. Prasterone is another drug recommended for relieving painful intercourse. It is available in the form of capsules that need to be placed inside the vagina every day to regulate hormonal balance and support natural vaginal lubrication.

Since the topically applied hormonal preparation goes directly into the vagina, it can help you avoid some of the systemic or general side effects of oral oestrogen pills. You may use these medications with other lubricants for additional benefits. Using lubricants would reduce pain by minimising friction.

Desensitisation Therapy

Desensitisation therapy involves learning exercises to induce vaginal relaxation. This therapy is suitable for women who suffer from painful sex due to severe stress and anxiety, or vaginismus caused due to the spasms of the muscles. Desensitisation therapy would inhibit the contractions of the muscles by training these muscles to relax, thereby reducing pain.

Sex Therapy And Counselling

Suppose painful sex is severe to the extent that it starts affecting your routine life or creates other mental or physical health issues. In that case, your doctor may recommend sex therapy and counselling to avoid further complications. When sexual intercourse has been painful for a long time, women tend to have a negative emotional response to any form of sexual stimulation.

The response may range from anger, irritability and frustration, to depression and destructive tendencies. Suppose you and your partner have been avoiding sexual intimacy due to painful intercourse, you may need help from an expert, psychiatrist, psychologist, or counsellor to improve communication and restore intimacy.

Talking to the counsellor or therapist would help resolve emotional issues and enable you to derive better results with the medications or other treatments you are receiving. Cognitive behavioural therapy (CBT) is often a part of the counselling that your doctor may recommend to change your negative thought patterns and behaviour.

Moisturisers

Medicated moisturisers may help to reduce friction during intercourse, just like lubricants. However, moisturisers can penetrate your skin more effectively than lubricants, so the effect of moisturisers usually lasts longer. Hence, if you suffer from severe dryness of the vagina, you may apply a medicated moisturiser such as Replens. It would keep working for three to four days and maintain adequate moisturisation in the vaginal tissues, thereby relieving pain during intercourse.

Oral Oestrogen Pills

If oestrogen creams and inserts do not help to reduce pain, your gynaecologist might recommend oral medications like oestrogen pills. Hormonal therapy may help provide relief from painful intercourse and other symptoms of menopause, like hot flushes, mood swings, and increased sweating.

The use of these medications and treatments could be beneficial for restoring pleasure in your sexual life. It would help you avoid pain and restore sexual intimacy between you and your partner.

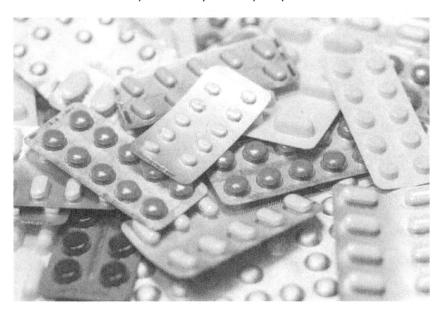

Chapter 6
Key To An Abundant Sexual Life

Alternative Therapy System

The Alternative Therapy System is a guide to the comprehensive alternative therapies you may opt to try. But it is important, however, to read through the whole section and get the full information. Subsequently, the system will serve as a shortcut to the key action points. You may experiment or try all of them out and see which works best for you. Thereafter, you can make more effective use of the system and empower yourself to get the ultimate results through regular practice, and in no time you will be living your dream of a sexually fulfilling life.

This system has two parts:
1. Exercises
2. Therapies

A. Exercise:
- **Child Pose**
- **Happy Baby Pose**
- **Breathing**
- **Pelvic Floor Exercise**
- **Aerobic**

Alternative Therapy System: Exercise

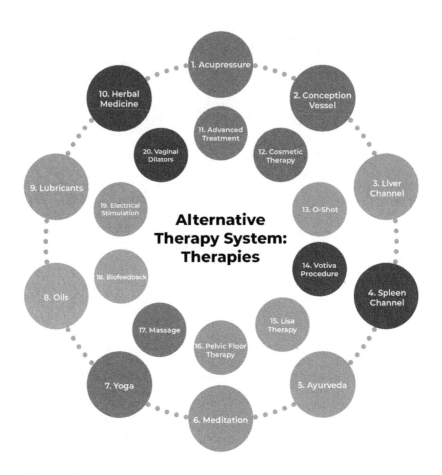

B. Therapies:

- **Acupressure**
- **Conception Vessel**
- **Liver Channel**
- **Spleen Channel**
- **Ayurveda**
- **Meditation**
- **Yoga**
- **Oils**
- **Lubricants**
- **Herbal Medicine**
- **Advanced Treatment**
- **Cosmetic Therapy**
- **O-Shot**

- **Votiva Procedure**
- **Lisa Therapy**
- **Pelvic Floor Therapy**
- **Massage**
- **Biofeedback**
- **Electrical Stimulation**
- **Vaginal Dilators**

If you think you are going through a rough phase in life due to painful intercourse, you can set aside your worries because it is completely possible to avoid this problem even without any medications or conventional treatments.

Yes, if you are not yet ready to visit a gynaecologist, you can try alternative therapies that can help you get rid of pain during intercourse safely and effectively.

Alternative therapies form the crux of our conventional or modern system of medicine. Alternative therapies like physiotherapy, Ayurveda, herbal remedies, yoga, meditation, acupressure, and acupuncture are considered safe for managing a variety of illnesses and painful sex is, luckily, one of them.

Let's take a look at some of the most effective alternative therapies specifically recommended for women who suffer from pain during intercourse.

Exercises For Painful Sex

Physiotherapy involves exercises, both active and passive. These exercises aim to strengthen the muscles in the affected part to provide relief from your symptoms.

Women who suffer from pain during intercourse should perform exercises focused on the muscles of the lower pelvic region. The spasm of the pelvic floor muscles, abdominal muscles, and vaginal muscles can play a role in triggering painful intercourse.

The weakness of these muscles can also be one of the reasons for the pain experienced during intercourse. Exercises can strengthen these muscles while preventing excessive contractions, thus relieving this condition. Some of the best exercises for managing pain during sex are discussed below.

Child Pose

The first step in the Alternative Therapy System to avoid painful intercourse is to lay more emphasis on the muscles in the pelvic floor. The Child Pose can help stretch out the pelvic region muscles and prevent spasms. It is a very simple exercise that you can perform at any time.

To practise, kneel down and bring your arms forward to reach the knees. Then, touch the ground while taking slow and deep breaths. Stay in this pose for 20 to 30 seconds, and release. Repeat the same 10 to 15 times. You can practise this pose once or twice a day. Over a few weeks, the pelvic floor muscles will strengthen and relax and help you avoid painful intercourse.

Happy Baby Pose

Here's another exercise that could help reduce spasms of the muscles in your hips and pelvic region.

To practise, lie down on a mat and bring the knees to touch your belly. Breathe in slowly and lift the legs up as much as possible. While doing so, bring the arms close to touch the legs. Hold this pose for about 30 seconds and then release. Repeat the same 10 to 15 times.

You can practise this pose once or twice a day. This will help the pelvic floor muscles to relax, prevent their contractions or spasms, and relieve painful sex.

Diaphragmatic Breathing

Breathing is an involuntary process. Several muscles in the body take part in breathing. Even though we are unaware of our breathing it continues day and night, even while we are sleeping. However, breathing can play a huge role in providing relief from pain during intercourse, as well as pain and discomfort caused due to other conditions like arthritis.

Breathing exercises involve making conscious or voluntary efforts to involve your diaphragm during inhalation or exhalation. The diaphragm is like a huge sheet of muscles that rests between the chest and the abdomen. It moves down while inhaling and moves up during exhaling with alternate contraction and relaxation of the muscles it is made of.

To perform a diaphragmatic breathing exercise, you need to focus your attention on the diaphragm while breathing in and out very slowly. To practise, place your right hand on the chest and your left hand on the belly. Take in slow deep breaths while focusing on the diaphragm.

As you breathe in slowly the diaphragm is pushed down, giving the pelvis enough time to relax and stretch. Do this for at least five minutes every day. You may increase the duration of diaphragmatic breathing exercises as you are able to control the contractions and relaxation of these muscles more efficiently.

Practising this exercise regularly would relax the pelvic muscles and prevent anxiety and spasms responsible for painful sex. You can also practice diaphragmatic breathing before and during sex to derive better benefits.

Kegel Exercises

No list of exercises for relieving problems related to the pelvic floor muscles would be complete without Kegel exercises. Kegel exercises are trusted to be one of the most effective ways to relax the muscles in the pelvic floor, lower abdomen, vagina, and cervix. It may also help to open up the vaginal canal during intercourse. Kegel exercises may improve the blood flow through the vulva and vagina, and help these tissues get sufficiently lubricated. This can help reduce pain during intercourse and make the experience more satisfying and enjoyable.

To begin with, you will have to locate the muscles of the lower abdomen and pelvic floor by stopping the stream of urine a few times during urination. The muscles that you clench while avoiding the passage of urine are the ones you need to focus on. To perform this exercise, simply hold these muscles for a few seconds and then relax. Repeat 10 to 15 times, twice or thrice a day.

Aerobic Exercises

Miracles can occur when you put in effort in the right direction! If you want to get rid of painful sex, you first need to improve your mental and physical health and maintain a healthy weight. The best exercises for painful sex, which actually work no less than a miracle, are aerobic exercises.

Aerobic exercises can take care of multiple causes of pain during intercourse, including obesity, polycystic ovarian disease, mental stress, anxiety, diabetes, and vascular disorders that affect the blood supply to the vagina. The drastic improvement to your sexual pleasure could be brought about just by taking a brisk walk for thirty to forty minutes a day, or performing other aerobic exercises such as running swimming, or cycling.

And how about taking your spouse with you when you go for a walk? This would surely bring you closer to each other and take you several steps ahead in your journey from painful sex to orgasms!

Acupressure Against Painful Intercourse

Let's now focus on acupuncture and acupressure points that you can use by yourself and with your partner to avoid painful intercourse and enhance your sex life.

Acupressure involves applying pressure on specific body points linked to specific organs and tissues. Most acupressure points are located on the palms and soles. However, acupressure points are also present on other skin parts, including your belly, thighs, neck, and arms. Applying pressure on each of these points would help to stimulate the normal functions of the specific tissues each is linked to and restore optimum health. Acupuncture works in a similar way. However, it involves inserting needles in those specific points instead of applying pressure.

Both acupressure and acupuncture are considered safe for the management of painful sex. However, it is advisable to first try acupressure, especially if you are already stressed and are experiencing pain. Acupuncture may not be suitable for you at this moment as injecting the points with needles may further worsen your stress and anxiety.

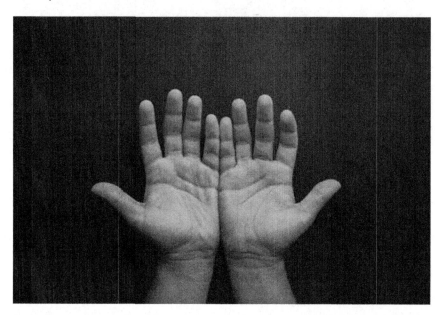

Here are some acupressure points you can try to relieve painful sex.

The Conception Vessel

The Conception Vessel refers to an acupressure point that is commonly used to enhance sexual pleasure. Most people think that this point can only be used to treat infertility or improve the chances of conception. However, contrary to its name, The Conception Vessel is not meant just for conception.

It can help to improve overall sexual satisfaction by enhancing lubrication in the vagina and reducing spasms of the pelvic muscles, thereby providing relief from painful sex. The Ren Channel is an acupuncture channel that runs along the midline of your body, beginning at Ren 1 and ending at Ren 24, near the chin.

Let's check the locations of points Ren 1, Ren 2, and Ren 6 on this channel that can help you in the management of painful sex.

- Ren 1 is a point midway between your labia and anus. This point can calm your stressed mind and soul, reduce genital pain and support vaginal lubrication.

- Ren 2 is situated along the midline of the body at your lower abdomen and the upper part of the pubic bone. The pubic bone might be just below your pubic hairline. This acupressure point helps to address the dryness of the vagina, reduces pain in the vagina caused due to spasms, and enhances sexual desire. Hence, it is suitable for women who suffer from low libido due to hormonal fluctuations occurring during mental stress, pregnancy, or menopause.

- Ren 6, also called the 'Sea of Qi', lies on the midline of the body, about two fingers below your belly button.

Applying gentle pressure on these points would stimulate the glands and tissues that play a role in sexual intercourse. It would help to restore a favourable balance of hormones in your body, thereby reducing stress and anxiety while stimulating sexual arousal.

The Liver Channel

The liver is considered an organ system in Chinese medicine. It plays a key role in the smooth flow of energy and blood in your body. The liver points 3 and 5 are considered vital in the management of painful intercourse.

- Liver 3 is situated in the web between your first and second toes. Applying pressure on this point could be great for relieving sexual frustration, spasming of vaginal muscles, and depression.

- Liver 5 is another acupressure point located about a hand's breadth and two more fingers above your ankle bone, just behind the tibia. This acupressure point would help to reduce pain and discomfort in the genitals related to infections.

The Spleen Channel

The spleen can help us with health issues such as fatigue, weakness, heaviness in the limbs, abdominal distention, and muscle weakness. It is in charge of converting the food we eat into a usable source of energy to ensure all cells and tissues of the body receive fuel to perform their functions.

Weakness or inefficient functioning of the spleen could reduce your energy levels and cause hormonal imbalance, due to which you may have irregular periods, polycystic ovarian disease, and painful sex. Spleen 6 could be the perfect acupressure point for addressing these issues.

The Spleen 6 point is situated about four fingers above and along the inner side of your ankle. Applying pressure on the Spleen 6 point may also help to ease painful intercourse and painful periods in women. You can use these acupressure points on yourself. Apply pressure on these points using your fingers for 30 to 60 seconds on a daily basis.

You may also ask your partner to apply pressure. It would surely bring you closer to each other and improve love and affection. Also, instead of simply applying pressure to these points, you may also try to massage the parts using your favourite massage oils. You may use essential oils like lavender and passionflower to enjoy the benefits of acupressure while deriving the soothing effects of these natural remedies.

Some couples have confessed that trying acupressure during sex can also help to relieve anxiety. It shifts the focus from pain to pleasure, especially when painful sex occurs due to mental stress. You can try massaging the acupressure points on the lower abdomen or legs during sex for added benefits.

Ayurveda

Ayurveda is an ancient system of medicine that originated in India. It aims to bring about a marked improvement in your physical, mental, and spiritual health with its holistic healing approach. Ayurveda focuses on eliminating impurities from your body to reduce the symptoms of painful sex. It can restore the optimum health of all body organs, including your vagina, ovaries, uterus, heart, lungs, and the brain, to allow all these organs to work in a synchronised manner during sexual activity. It can reduce vaginal dryness, mental stress, and anxiety. Ayurveda may also help to correct the hormonal imbalances occurring during pregnancy, breastfeeding, and menopause.

It may help to regulate the secretion of female reproductive hormones – oestrogen and progesterone – and even stress hormones like cortisol, and feel-good hormones like dopamine and serotonin. This would induce a favourable balance of hormones in the body and help women avoid the common factors responsible for painful sex. Women who suffer from painful sex are advised to practice Ayurveda regularly to achieve long-term results. It would not just reduce pain during intercourse, but also improve their sexual and reproductive health.

Meditation

If fear and anxiety are the reasons why you are not able to enjoy sex, you can try meditation to allay these negative emotions. Meditation can induce mental and physical relaxation and help you feel calm. It can reduce the contractions of the muscles in the vagina during intercourse and prevent painful intercourse.

Meditation is an art that can allow you to enter a state of improved consciousness and build your internal energy. Whenever you feel stressed, anxious, or irritated, practising meditation for a couple of minutes and focusing on yourself will allow you to leave the rest of the world aside for a moment and restore a sense of ease.

This would allow you to indulge yourself in a higher level of energy, optimism, and a positive attitude. You can include meditation in your daily routine and practice it for just twenty to thirty minutes every day to experience the change within yourself! It will help you feel fresh and relaxed, improve your sexual desire, and allow you to avoid painful spasms of the muscles during intercourse.

Yoga

Yoga is an integral part of Ayurveda that involves practising different poses, also called asanas. These yoga poses aim to stretch and strengthen different groups of muscles in your body. A five-minute yoga session every day can help relax the muscles in the vagina and help you avoid pain during intercourse.

You can practise the stretching sessions prior to intercourse to induce physical relaxation. Yoga can also have a positive influence on your mental and emotional health. It can heal a stressed mind and allow you to feel calm and relaxed at all times, including before and during intercourse.

Practising yoga on a regular basis would strengthen the muscles in the vagina and cervix and remove the tightness or stiffness of these muscles, thereby reducing pain and spasms associated with painful sex.

Ayurvedic Herbs

Ayurveda recommends using medicinal herbs to manage acute and chronic ailments, including painful sex. Women who suffer from severe mental stress and anxiety can use herbs such as brahmi to relieve these symptoms.

The use of shatavari and ashwagandha has been recommended for correcting hormonal imbalances responsible for painful sex. These herbs can also improve reproductive and menstrual dysfunctions, infertility, PCOD, endometriosis, premenstrual syndrome, amenorrhea, and dysmenorrhea, and offer holistic improvement in women's health.

Natural Oils

Women can derive significant relief from painful sex by applying natural lubricants to the vagina before sex. The application of natural oils such as coconut oil, olive oil, and petroleum jelly would enhance the lubrication of the vaginal tissues and prevent pain caused due to dryness and friction.

The use of natural oils is specifically beneficial for women who suffer from painful sex due to dryness caused as a result of hormonal changes occurring during menopause, pregnancy, or breastfeeding. Women who suffer from painful sex due to stress or anxiety can also use this remedy to alleviate symptoms.

These oils can soothe the vaginal tissues. Coconut oil and olive oil have a tendency to trap moisture. They can keep the vaginal tissues elastic and well lubricated, thereby providing relief from muscle spasms that occur due to stress or anxiety. This can provide significant relief from painful sex.

This alternative therapy may also be helpful for women who are recovering from injuries or bruises in the vaginal region. They can apply a small quantity of coconut oil or olive oil on the vagina before sex to allow for the smooth penetration of the penis. It will minimise friction during sexual activity and prevent the worsening of injuries.

However, women who suffer from active bacterial, viral, or fungal infections in the vagina, vulva, or cervix should avoid applying any oil as it may worsen their symptoms. The use of coconut oil is specifically recommended for those who are getting into an intimate relationship for the first time and are afraid of pain during intercourse.

If the first experience of having sex is painful, a woman may have persistent anxiety that may prevent her from enjoying sex for several years. The fear of pain may resurface each time she is having sex, causing spasms of the vaginal muscles. This can only make matters worse, creating a vicious cycle.

Applying coconut oil before the first intercourse would allow smoother penetration of the penis into the vagina and prevent fears related to sex.

Water-Soluble Lubricants

The use of water-soluble creams and lubricants that are enriched with oestrogen may help in reducing the pain associated with sex. Water-based lubricants would lessen the friction caused during penetration and thus provide relief from pain felt during sexual activity.

Chinese Herbal Medicines

Chinese herbal medicines have been found to be effective in the management of painful sex. Medicinal mushrooms like chaga, cordyceps, and reishi are revered for their natural medicinal potential to relieve sexual difficulties in women as well as men.

These natural remedies have been highly recommended in Chinese medicine for women who experience pain during intercourse due to lack of vaginal lubrication, hormonal imbalances, and mental stress.

These mushrooms work in different ways and correct the underlying abnormalities to help women avoid pain during sex. These natural alternatives are not just effective but also safe to use. You can try these alternative methods to overcome pain during sex.

It is advisable to choose the best natural alternatives to reduce painful sex depending on the specific cause of the pain. Regular use of these natural remedies will help you enjoy sex for many years.

Chapter 7
Advanced Treatments And
Cosmetic Therapies For Painful Sex

In case home remedies, medications, and alternative therapies do not provide the desired results, there are other things you can try. Advancements in the medical field have led to the development of therapies and cosmetic treatments that can help you avoid pain during intercourse.

Let us take a look at some of the most effective advanced treatments recommended for women who suffer from painful sex.

O-Shot

If you suffer from severe pain during sex, your doctor may recommend treatment with the O-Shot. It refers to a form of treatment that involves injecting PRP or platelet-rich plasma directly into the vagina, clitoris, clitoral hood, or the other genital areas. PRP injections work by encouraging blood flow into these tissues.

It can also promote cell growth in the area, thereby rejuvenating tissues damaged due to infection, injury, or ageing. It would improve sensitivity during sex and help you avoid pain. Thus, PRP injections like O-Shot may help in improving sexual pleasure and orgasms. The injection can be effective as a standalone treatment for women suffering from painful sex. It can also be used in combination with other therapies for better results.

Votiva

Votiva refers to an advanced radio-frequency treatment that is aimed at correcting structural abnormalities in the vagina that could be responsible for causing pain. This therapy works at a cellular level. It is an intravaginal and extravaginal therapy, which means it works on the issues in the vagina while correcting the causes outside of these tissues.

It can help to provide relief from all types of vaginal pains, including vulvodynia. Votiva offers a comfortable, effective, and safe treatment for the rejuvenation and tightening of the vagina and labia without the need for surgery. This therapy is specifically recommended for women who suffer from painful sex due to the loss of vaginal elasticity and dryness as a result of ageing.

These changes are collectively referred to as vaginal atrophy. As age increases, the body undergoes a host of changes, ranging from the loss of collagen and elastin to reduced oestrogen production. The physical bruises or trauma caused during vaginal childbirth can only make the symptoms worse.

Votiva can reduce vaginal atrophy and the associated painful intercourse by stimulating the production of elastin and collagen, improving hormonal balance, and rejuvenating and healing damaged tissues.

Common Concerns That Can Be Managed With Votiva Include:

- Loss of elasticity or wrinkled appearance of the vulva and labia
- Loosened cervical and vaginal canal due to ageing or repeated vaginal deliveries
- Reduced vaginal lubrication
- Reduced sensitivity of the vagina
- Reduced blood flow through the vaginal tissues
- Pain caused due to labial hypertrophy
- Loss of sexual desire
- Loss of self-esteem due to age-related vaginal atrophy

Votiva uses advanced technologies including FractoraV and FormaV to address the internal and external vaginal areas of concern. FormaV causes gentle thermal tissue remodelling, while FractoraV results in the radio-frequency contraction of these tissues. Most women need around three sessions of Votiva to derive optimal results.

What makes Votiva one of the best advanced treatments for women with painful sex is that it is a non-surgical treatment that requires no incisions or anaesthesia. It can be performed in the doctor's clinic on an out-patient basis.

Also, it does not leave any scars or cause any of the serious side effects potentially associated with anaesthesia or surgical procedures, like infection of a wound, for example.

Laser Therapy

Laser therapy offers innovative and highly effective treatment for women with severe painful intercourse, especially when caused by excessive dryness. It offers long-term solutions and helps them avoid complications related to painful intercourse, such as infertility and depression.

Besides eliminating vaginal dryness, laser therapy may also help slow down age-related vaginal atrophy by stimulating collagen and elastin production. It may also help to heal damaged tissues and restore healthy contractions of the muscles in the vaginal canal.

This can help regenerate the vaginal mucosa, support vaginal rejuvenation, restore optimum elasticity of the muscles, and thus provide relief from pain during sex. Most women need three sessions of laser therapy to ease the pain.

Pelvic Floor Therapy

Your physiotherapist may recommend pelvic floor therapy to strengthen the pelvic floor and the muscles of the lower abdomen. While most exercises for strengthening the pelvic floor muscles can be performed at home or in a doctor's clinic, some therapies are more intensive and need active intervention by an expert physiotherapist.
Some of the most effective pelvic floor therapies for managing painful sex are discussed below.

Massage

Women suffering from severe pain and sexual dysfunction may benefit from physiotherapy sessions that involve internal or external massage under the care of an expert therapist. During the internal massage, the physiotherapist would move the fingers up the vagina to identify trigger points that could be causing disturbances in the pelvic floor.

They would then try to dilate the vaginal canal by stretching these muscles internally to loosen them or prepare them for normal functioning.

Internal massage therapy may fix a wide range of problems, including pain and sexual discomfort, as well as myofascial pelvic pain.

Biofeedback

Biofeedback can be performed by your physiotherapist at their clinic. It typically involves placing sensors on the patient's abdomen and anal canal. These sensors are later connected to a computer and monitor how the muscles behave when the pelvic floor relaxes or contracts.

The 'feedback' or information received can be studied on the computer to identify irregularities in these muscle groups. Any specific issues detected can be addressed with appropriate exercises or other treatments.

Electrical Stimulation

This therapy is usually recommended for women who have severe weakness of the pelvic floor muscles and when physical exercises are less effective or stressful. Electrical stimulation involves winding a piece of a pad around the skin near the vagina. The pad is then stimulated with an electric current.

The resulting electrical stimulation can help the pelvic floor muscles to contract and expand, and loosen up, which is what happens when exercises are performed. This process can be performed in combination with biofeedback for better results.

Vaginal Dilators

Vaginal dilators offer one of the simplest and the most effective ways to stretch your pelvic floor muscles without the need of a doctor or a physiotherapist. Vaginal dilators are tube-like devices that can be inserted into the vagina, just like a tampon. These small devices need to be rotated gently to stretch the muscles in the vaginal walls.

It is advisable to perform this therapy about three to four times a week for about twenty to thirty minutes per session. It can help improve the flexibility and elasticity of the vagina and prevent tightening or stiffness of the muscles during sex, thereby providing relief from painful sex.

Women who suffer from severe pain during intercourse can consult their gynaecologist or physiotherapist to check which of these advanced therapies might be suitable for them. It will help them avoid painful intercourse and restore sexual satisfaction.

Chapter 8
Regimen To Combat Painful Sex

Your diet plays a key role in keeping you fit and healthy, and at the same time, it is very effective in your sexual health.

A healthy sex drive is dependent on being emotionally and physically fit. Hence, it is no surprise that most foods known to boost your sex life include nutritious choices.

A nutritious diet can benefit your sex life in several ways, such as:
- Boosting your libido
- Reducing mental stress
- Improving blood flow to the vagina

Here's a list of foods that would enhance your sexual desire, improve vaginal lubrication, and help you avoid painful intercourse.

Nuts And Seeds

Eating a handful of nuts and seeds once a day helps ensure your body receives a good supply of proteins that are needed for building stronger muscles. It would strengthen the muscles in the pelvic floor and help you avoid painful spasms during sex.

Apples

Apples contain a compound called quercetin that can act as a natural antioxidant. It is a type of flavonoid that can provide several health benefits to improve your sex life. Quercetin can help to improve blood circulation, lessen anxiety, and maintain hormonal balance, thereby reducing the risk of painful sex.

Oysters

You must have heard of the aphrodisiac effects of oysters. Oysters are high in minerals like zinc that would increase the blood flow through the vagina and improve lubrication.

Salmon

Salmon is known for its omega-3 fatty acids. Omega-3s help regulate the blood flow through the vagina and improve mental health by enhancing the secretion of feel-good hormones in the brain.

Beetroot

Just like apples, beetroot are rich in antioxidants and several vitamins. Eating them would enhance the iron content in your meals and prevent the deficiency of this vital nutrient.

Including beetroot in your regular meals would improve your general health and thus provide relief from sexual complaints.

Some other foods you can include in your regular diet to avoid painful sex and improve your sexual desire include:
- Walnuts
- Almonds
- Berries, such as strawberries, blueberries, and raspberries
- Watermelon
- Avocados
- Peaches
- Eggs
- Coffee
- Saffron

Making minor changes in your diet and ensuring your diet comprises all food groups including proteins, complex carbohydrates, and healthy fats, as well as vitamins, minerals, and dietary fibre, is key to improving your sexual life.

Real-Life Stories

Let me now share with you some real-life stories of women who have overcome painful sex and are now enjoying their sex life by adopting the healthy and effective practices discussed so far.

Read the stories as narrated by those who have gone through the painful experience. I have changed the names of the women and men to protect their privacy.

Sex: A Trauma?

Hi, I am Nancy. For me, sex was associated more with trauma than pleasure. I was on cloud nine when my best friend, Max, proposed marriage to me. Within a month, we got engaged and married in a grand ceremony. But my happiness didn't last long. The pain started from day one. How can I forget that night when we got closer to each other? It was our first time in spite of knowing each other for years. Believe me – I was quite excited for the moment.

But just as he was about to enter, I literally screamed. He was taken aback. But, he obliged. (I couldn't have found a better life partner!) What happened was that the moment he was to enter, I remembered what my friend had told me about HER first sexual experience and how painful it was. I was scared out of my wits. Unfortunately, this continued for several months. Max tried to pacify me and always assured me that he was with me.

I knew it wasn't right to avoid sex just because of what I had learned from my friend. But somehow, that sense of fear and anxiety was stuck in my mind. No matter how much I tried, it was impossible for me to be calm during sex. Luckily, Max's friend is a gynaecologist. We decided to consult her about these issues. She assured me there was nothing to worry about. She advised me to practice meditation for ten minutes after dinner and to use lubricants during sex.

She also advised me and Max to spend more time on foreplay to ease stress and induce arousal. These simple tricks worked wonders. Within a week or so, we had sex without any anxiety or pain but with lots of pleasure and satisfaction. I reached out to my friend after this and suggested that she should try the same things. I was so happy when she told me my suggestions had worked well and it brought her closer to her husband. It helped her solve the marital issues and conflicts she was having due to the lack of sexual pleasure and intimacy.

Why Now?

Hi, I am Martha. Let me share with you how my life changed after menopause. 'Why now?' This was the topmost question in my mind at that time. I had never before had any issues with sex. My husband and I had always experimented with different positions and loved the intimacy that helped us forget our worries and day-to-day stress.

But, later, as I entered menopause, the picture began to change. I noticed that I would get angry at him even if he was just trying to kiss me. I also used to get irritated when he was touching me, and often pushed him away. And sex? That was impossible! I could feel his penis hurting me.

Was I going to accept it as a part of life, accept that this is now how things are? No! I started working on it, beginning with, 'why should it happen?' After doing some research, I consulted my family physician. He confirmed what I had learned, and told me that it was possibly due to hormonal change.

He advised me to try HRT (hormone replacement therapy) and suggested other strategies like doing pelvic floor exercises, physiotherapy, using lubricants, and massage. I felt an improvement in my mood and sexual arousal within a few weeks. As time went on, I felt the desire to get closer and have some moments of intimacy.

We had sex again! And it was just like it used to be! No pain, no anger, no irritability! Just orgasms! I strongly recommend to all women to be aware of how menopause affects their physical, mental, and sexual health and seek the right treatment to avoid issues that can be easily avoided by simply trying what worked for me.

Love Or Sex?

I was trapped between the love for my wife and my desire to have sex. Hi, I am Stephen by the way. I love my wife, Annabeth, very much and didn't want to hurt her in any way. But at the same time, I was feeling deprived of sex. Annabeth often complained of pain during sex, and this kept us from getting intimate.

After struggling a lot with the dilemma, I decided the best way was not 'love OR sex' but 'love AND sex'. I decided to help Annabeth overcome her symptoms of pain so that both of us would be able to enjoy good sex. I remember my friend discussing similar issues he had with his girlfriend.

He had told me how physiotherapy and yoga had helped her overcome the pain. I decided to follow the same approach and taught my wife how to perform pelvic floor exercises. We also used vaginal dilators to ease spasms in the vaginal canal.

Over a period of time, Annabeth seemed to be more comfortable with the vaginal dilators and didn't complain of pain. We tried sex but without much penetration. And it was successful. She didn't have as much pain as before. We continued the same treatment and started using lubricants during sex.

Within a month or so, things changed from her trying to avoid me to trying to get closer. I had won the love of my wife and also showed her that sex is beautiful!

Time To Take Action

If you suffer from painful sex there is no need to panic or feel anxious. It is a very common condition and you are not alone having these issues. Instead of feeling sad or avoiding sex, identifying and eliminating the cause of painful sex would be a better way to manage this problem.

It should be noted that most of the recommendations can only be done under the supervision of a qualified professional. Follow the remedies we have discussed in this book to avoid pain during sex, so that you can enjoy your intimate moments with your loved one for years after years.

Chapter 9
Achieving Orgasm

Now that I have guided you on how to overcome painful intercourse, it is time to focus on getting regular orgasms.

If you have already managed to overcome pain during sex with the help of the tips and treatments we've discussed so far, let's move on to the next step of learning how you can enjoy sex to the fullest and then get a good orgasm.

Orgasm Multiplier System

The Orgasm Multiplier System gives you an overview of the steps and actions you need to take to get your desired results. You will learn the different types of orgasm. This system will give you a quick understanding of each type of orgasm and how to get the maximum benefit from each. The different types of orgasms are clitoral orgasm, vaginal orgasm, cervical orgasm, nipple orgasm, G-spot orgasm, and combination orgasm.

Female Orgasms

A female orgasm is a highly pleasurable experience that occurs during sexual activity or masturbation. Female orgasms serve several important purposes. The pleasure they can bring can encourages you to have sex more often.

This, in turn, can promote your emotional and physical well-being, and can create a positive impact on your relationship with your partner – which may lead to improving the chances of conception, when it is desired. Having said that, it doesn't mean that having orgasms makes women more likely to become pregnant.

No, it doesn't work that way. If you do not want to get pregnant, you can still enjoy sex using appropriate contraceptives, so that you can enjoy an orgasm without the fear of getting pregnant. However, there are huge benefits attached to achieving orgasms for women who are trying to conceive.

The lack of pain and improved pleasure during sex can allow them to have sex more often and for longer. Moreover, the pleasure women can get from having orgasms can improve their emotional health and reduce stress. This would help in preventing hormonal disturbances and enhance reproductive health.

It is the effect of orgasms that can increase your chances of conception. Hence, if you are trying to get pregnant, focusing on getting orgasms could be an effective way to attain your goal.

What Happens During A Female Orgasm?

A female orgasm occurs after arousal when the blood flows into the genitals, especially the clitoris, causing it to become highly sensitive to touch. As arousal increases, your heart rate, breathing rate, and blood pressure also increase. And as orgasm approaches, the muscles in the vagina start to spasm or twitch. Most women also experience rhythmic spasms of the muscles in the vagina as the orgasm approaches.

The sexual response in women follows specific stages, as explained below:
- Sexual excitement, that helps to build arousal

- Plateau, when the sexual arousal has increased to a point where it levels off
- An orgasm that causes an intense feeling of pleasure and satisfaction
- Resolution, after which arousal slowly diminishes

The stages may differ among different women. However, they tend to follow a similar pattern, with the arousal increasing slowly and then declining after orgasm has been achieved.

Most females are able to get another orgasm after the stage of resolution, whereas men often require a period of rest before they can have another orgasm.

What Are The Health Benefits Of Having Orgasms?

There is no doubt that orgasms are intensely pleasurable and pleasure, of course, has its own benefits. Pleasurable sex with great orgasms can improve your mood, boost immunity, relieve stress, and foster personal relationships. As mentioned earlier, you do not have to get orgasms to become pregnant.

However, orgasms might support the body's metabolic rate and help with your digestion, fat loss, energy levels, and much more. Though there are several benefits attached to female orgasms, there are also many misconceptions that often prevent women from getting there.

Before we learn the best ways to get an orgasm, let us first clear the myths and misconceptions associated with female orgasms so that you get a clear idea of what it means.

Common Misconceptions Related To Female Orgasms

Women Cannot Have Vaginal Orgasms

This is one of the most common myths about female orgasms. Most men and even women believe that women can not have vaginal orgasms. It is agreed that vaginal orgasms are far less common than those arising from clitoral or nipple stimulation. Yet, it would be wrong to assume that women can not have vaginal orgasms. Some women can have them, usually with other forms of sexual stimulation.

The fact is that female orgasms may result from several types of stimulation, like clitoral, vaginal, and nipple contact, and not every orgasm occurs from the same type of sexual arousal.

A Woman Needs To Be In Love To Get An Orgasm

It is commonly believed that a woman can get orgasms only if she is in love with the partner. It should be noted however that orgasms involve complex biological and psychological mechanisms. Hence, experiencing an orgasm may not be the same for all women.

Some women might need to feel loved to be able to get an orgasm, but others may not. Hence, it is wrong to assume that women must be in love to get an orgasm. The relationship of the woman with the partner may or may not influence her ability to get an orgasm during sex.

In fact, she is more likely to get orgasms more frequently if:
- The foreplay was longer
- There was sufficient nipple or clitoris stimulation
- There is more oral sex
- She is asked what she wants in bed
- There is an engagement in sexual calls or emails before sex
- She has acted out sexual fantasies or expressed love before or during sex
- She has tried new and exciting sexual positions

A Partner Can Tell When A Woman Has Had An Orgasm

Most men and women believe that it is possible for the partner to know when the woman has had an orgasm. However, this is not true. While some women make noises such as groaning when they get an orgasm, some may be silent. Also, some women tend to flush and sweat after getting an orgasm, but not all women do.

This is why it is not possible for the partner to know when the woman has had an orgasm. Now that we have cleared the misconceptions related to female orgasms, let's have a look at the different types of orgasms and the best ways to achieve them.

Types Of Orgasms:

Clitoral Orgasm

Clitoral orgasm, as the name suggests, is in the clitoris. There are several ways to make the most of clitoral orgasm. These are shown in the clitoral orgasm system below.

Clitoral Orgasm System:
1. **Direct Stimulation**
2. **Indirect Stimulation**
3. **Rubbing**
4. **Caressing**
5. **Rubbing - Varied Directions**
6. **Pressure**
7. **Frequency**
8. **Penis Stroking**

Clitoral orgasms involve sexual arousal with direct or indirect stimulation of the small projection present at the upper anterior part of the vaginal opening, called the clitoris. It is also considered the penis for women. As your partner gently rubs the clitoris for a few seconds, you will be able to feel the sensation building as your pleasure increases and peaks slowly. To try clitoral orgasms, ask your partner to rub or caress the clitoris with his palm, the tips of fingers, or even a small vibrator.

Make sure your clitoris is wet or slightly lubricated. Your partner can begin by rubbing it in an up and down or side to side manner. Once it begins to feel good, ask him to rub faster and apply harder pressure by stroking it in a repetitive motion. Applying more pressure and frequency to the motion can help to intensify the pleasure, thus taking you over the edge. While your partner fondles your clitoris, you can stroke his penis to arouse him. Caress the penis to make him feel loved and want to be loved. Once both of you feel aroused, let him enter you. Hold him and love him as he strokes in and out slowly until you get an orgasm, and he ejaculates.

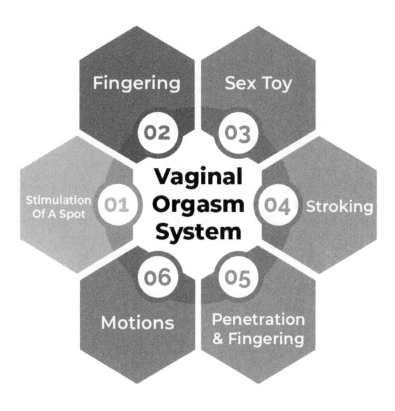

Vaginal Orgasm System

Vaginal orgasm could be obtained with these steps: stimulation of the A-spot, fingering, sex toy stimulation, stroking, penetration and various motions. A complete understanding of the system is required for you to use the system effectively. Please read and follow the system step by step and thereafter it will become easy and quick to use.

Vaginal Orgasm System:
- **Stimulation of A-spot**
- **Fingering**
- **Sex Toy**
- **Stroking**
- **Penetration and Fingering**
- **Various Motions**

Very few women are able to climax or get an orgasm with vaginal stimulation alone. Vaginal orgasms could be obtained with the stimulation of the front of the vaginal wall that is also home to the A-spot, which is actually the anterior fornix. Stimulating the A-spot can result in intense lubrication and more satisfying orgasms.

To get vaginal orgasms, ask your partner to rub the part with his finger or even a sex toy. He can even stroke the vagina with his penis as he enters you. Since the pleasure and arousal come from the walls of the vagina, he can try experimenting with the width. He can do this by inserting one or two fingers along the sides of his penis, into your vagina.

He can also stimulate the A-spot by focusing pressure on the anterior (front) wall of the vagina as he slides his fingers and/or penis in and out. He can continue with the motion and pressure that feels best to you, to let the arousal and pleasure mount until it reaches the peak.

Cervical Orgasm System

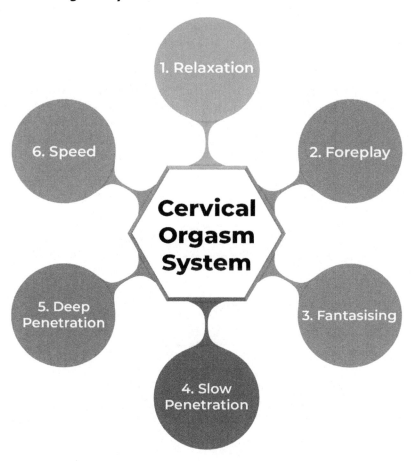

Cervical Orgasm System:

The Cervical Orgasm System begins with relaxation and can end in the most intense orgasm for a woman.
- **Relaxation**
- **Foreplay**
- **Fantasising**
- **Slow Penetration**
- **Deep Penetration**
- **Speed**

Cervical stimulation has immense potential that can lead to a full-body orgasm, in that it sends waves of tingly sexual pleasure from your head to your toes. Cervical orgasms can keep on giving you intense sexual pleasure lasting longer than the other forms of orgasms. It is also the best orgasm that you can enjoy during intercourse when he enters his penis into your vagina. To try cervical orgasms, lie down feeling relaxed yet aroused.

Some foreplay magic and indulging in sexual fantasies can arouse you and your partner further while he rubs your clitoris. Your partner can start off slow, as he enters his penis into the vagina, working his way deeper into the cervix gradually while you guide him to the depth that feels the best. Ask him to keep at it to allow the pleasure to build.

Nipple Orgasm System

Nipple Orgasm System

01 Caress Breasts

02 Squeeze Nipples

03 Tease

04 Pleasure

05 Penetration

Nipple Orgasm System:

The nipples play a key role in orgasm generally but are key to nipple orgasm, from caressing the breasts to squeezing the nipples to teasing and pleasure and penetration. Follow the recommended system step by step and you will love it.

1. **Caress breasts**
2. **Squeeze nipples**
3. **Tease**
4. **Pleasure**
5. **Penetration**

Your nipples have a rich supply of nerve endings that can provide intense pleasure when played with. When stimulated, the nipples can set ablaze the genital centres of sexual pleasure. It can light up the same part of the brain that tends to get stimulated during vaginal and clitoral stimulation.

Your partner can start with squeezing and caressing your breasts or other parts of the body, while avoiding touching the nipples. He can then move on to teasing your nipples by tracing the areola with his fingertips until you feel turned on. Let him show your nipples lots of love by pinching or rubbing them until you attain maximum pleasure.

Let him hold and squeeze your breasts or pinch your nipples during intercourse. He can hold your breasts in both the 'man on top' or the 'woman on top' positions to ensure both of you get immense pleasure and intense orgasms.

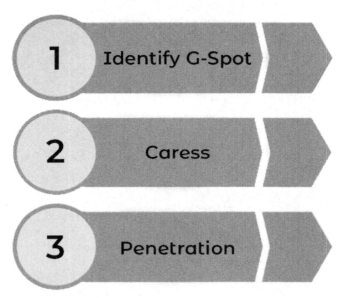

G-Spot Orgasm System

1. Identify G-Spot

2. Caress

3. Penetration

G-Spot Orgasm System

Identifying the G-spot is key to getting G-spot orgasms. G-spot orgasm can be very enjoyable and great fun. Follow the system carefully and reach greater heights of pleasure.

G-Spot Orgasm System:

- **Identify G-Spot**
- **Caress**
- **Penetration**

The G-spot is the area located along the front wall of the vagina. For most women, it can create an intense wet orgasm once stimulated.

This part can be stimulated when your partner rubs it gently with his fingers or the G-spot vibrator. Try this for a few minutes before he enters his penis into the vagina to enhance natural lubrication and get better orgasms.

Combination Of Orgasms

Couples can also try to achieve a combo orgasm by pleasuring the clitoris and vagina simultaneously. The result would be a powerful climax and an intense pleasure that can be felt inside and out.

To try this, let your partner rub the clitoris and the front wall of the vagina using both his hands before he slides his penis in the vagina. He can also use vibrators to stimulate the vagina and clitoris at the same time for mastering the combo orgasm. Let him stroke his penis in and out to build the pleasure. Rubbing of the clitoris during the thrusting movement of the penis will heighten the pleasure further.

Here are some steps you can follow:
- **Rub Clitoris**
- **Rub A-Spot**
- **Vibrator Stimulation**
- **Motions**
- **Rub Clitoris**
- **Rub Nipples**

What Happens To The Body When You Get An Orgasm?

Every woman is different, and so is her response to orgasm. Some orgasms are more intense and last longer, while others are less intense and last for a very short period. Some tend to be wetter than others.

In spite of these differences, there are some changes that typically occur in the body during an orgasm, such as:
1. Rapid contractions of the muscles in the vagina
2. Experiencing involuntary contractions of the muscles in other parts of the body, such as the legs and abdomen
3. Increase in heart rate, blood pressure, and breathing rate

You might find it a bit difficult to achieve orgasm the first few times you try, but once you get the hang of it, it will be much easier for you to achieve it. You can experiment with the different types of orgasm to enhance the pleasure and get the most out of this unique and intensely satisfying experience.

Chapter 10
Tips To Get Better Orgasms

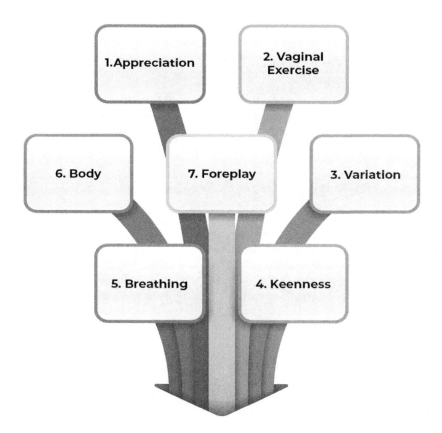

Supporting Techniques:

- **Vaginal Exercise**
- **Variation**
- **Keenness**
- **Breathing**
- **Body**
- **Foreplay**

In women, orgasms follow a characteristic build-up of muscle tension, with an increase in the blood flow to the genitals, causing a sensation of remarkable sexual pleasure.

If you are already excited at the thought of getting orgasms, read further to learn the best tips that would make your orgasms stronger and more satisfying.

Focus On Breathing

You can take slow physical and emotional steps to make an effortless attempt to get better orgasms and make the climax more intense and steadier. Focusing your attention on your breathing pattern is an effective step that could intensify your orgasms.

You will be astonished to see the remarkable difference that a change in your breathing pattern from deep and slow to quick and short can make to your sexual excitement. By taking quick short breaths you will be able to get stronger orgasms, as this form of breathing also increases the heart rate, so creating a state of sexual arousal.

Know Your Body

Another excellent way to get stronger orgasms is to make yourself familiar with your own body. It is common for women to fail to get an orgasm simply because they have never considered learning the characteristics that can arouse and awaken them sexually during physical activity.

If you want to get better orgasms, pay attention to the kind of touch that can give you maximum pleasure and the feeling of satisfaction. Moreover, do not feel nervous while expressing the things you like the most during sex to your partner. Guide him to do what stimulates you by gently taking his hands to the parts of your body where his touch would help you feel aroused.

Lengthier Foreplay

One of the common reasons for not attaining an orgasm is the failure to spend enough time on foreplay. The mind and body of a woman undergo multifaceted variations during the preparation for intended sexual activity. These modifications help to assist in avoiding pain and distress during sex, and increase their pleasure and the possibility of an intense orgasm.

This normally takes about ten to fifteen minutes to occur. This indicates that women need at least ten minutes of foreplay to be prepared for sexual intimacy. Stimulation of genitals and nipples, oral sex, and deep and intense kissing can amplify a woman's chances of getting an orgasm.

This is why couples are advised to spend enough time on foreplay to improve their sexual satisfaction and get better orgasms.

Appreciate Your Body

Contrary to popular belief, getting an orgasm has nothing to do with how you look. Every woman can get an orgasm regardless of how she looks, her skin tone, her body weight, and other issues related to her appearance. Hence, the key to getting strong orgasms is to love your body, especially those parts where you feel more aroused when touched.

If you do not love your body, you might end up thinking more about your appearance during intercourse than being in the moment of feeling and relishing sensual arousal. Worrying about your body's perceived flaws will only hinder your sexual response. Hence, if you want to enjoy sex, focus on how you feel.

Focus on each and every sensation that you experience, including your breathing and muscle contractions, instead of thinking about how you look.

Vaginal Exercises

Working out the muscles surrounding the vagina could improve the supply of blood to your genitals and help to build up stimulation. Kegel exercises are the best for working out the muscles in the genitals and pelvic floor. You can practice Kegel exercises regularly to improve your orgasms and enhance your sexual pleasure.

Women who are more proficient in contracting and relaxing the muscles in the vagina and pelvic floor are able to boost the sexual pleasure of their partner as well and bring him to orgasm too. Men can also practice exercises to strengthen their pelvic floor muscles to improve their orgasms, get healthier erections, and be able to satisfy their partner.

Try Different Positions

You may find your sexual routine becomes repetitive with time. It can make the whole experience more predictable and even boring. This is why couples are advised to experiment with different sexual positions to introduce novelty and excitement to their sexual activity.

It is important to break from the routine and try different sexual positions to get better orgasms. You can try the woman on top position or the doggy style position to improve your orgasms. You can also consider experimenting with other positions in order to find what suits you the best.

Build Sexual Keenness

It is good to feel aroused in a moment while watching a sensual video or reading an erotic novel. However, if you want to plan an exciting sexual activity, it will definitely help to build arousal slowly throughout the day. You can get your sensual feelings to develop and flow into an erotic longing by planning and imagining the experience throughout the day.

Things you can do include sending suggestive text messages to your partner, teasing each other, being open to erotic talks, or wearing a sexy outfit in anticipation of sex. All of this would lead to an upsurge in your arousal and enhance you and your partner's prospects of getting very strong orgasms.

Orgasm is the ultimate pleasure you can derive from a sexual activity. You can enjoy sex and get better orgasms by simply following the tips and tricks we've discussed here. It will intensify your sexual pleasure and make your orgasms stronger. Getting an orgasm is what will make having sex more desirable for you.

It is the orgasms that will make you want to get closer to your partner and have sex more often. It is also the orgasms that will make you love yourself and your body. So, it would be unfair if you were to deprive yourself of these benefits. You need to guide yourself and your partner by experimenting with what feels the best and what arouses you the most.

Chapter 11
Best Time Of Your Life: Super Orgasms
A Step-By-Step Guide

Orgasms are great. But getting a super orgasm is altogether a different level of pleasure! When you can get super orgasms and an unmatchable level of sexual gratification, why should you content yourself with simple orgasms?

If you agree, keep reading to know what super orgasms mean and the step-by-step method to achieve them.

What Are Super Orgasms?

So, what exactly is a super orgasm, and how does it happen biologically? Some women describe super orgasms as the orgasms that come continuously in the forms of waves that stay longer and feel more intense than typical orgasms. Some women report continuous repeat-orgasms as a kind of orgasm that feels ten times more pleasurable than the common orgasm, to the point when you can actually say it is close to getting a super orgasm!

Super orgasms and multiple orgasms are pretty similar; though not exactly the same. The key difference between multiple orgasms and the super orgasms is the number of orgasms achieved consecutively during the session. Getting multiple orgasms means reaching climax two or three times while, with super orgasms, it can be up to ten to twenty times. So, are you ready to know how to achieve super orgasms?

How To Get Super Orgasms

How can you achieve super orgasms? Super orgasm is achievable within these seven steps. With the right kind of stimulation at the right spot, you will master the art of getting super orgasms. Some women need both G-spot and clitoral stimulation to get a super orgasm. Before we proceed, let me first explain how to find your clitoris.

How To Find The Clitoris

Most women need clitoral stimulation to get orgasms. The clitoris is a tiny nub packed with a rich supply of nerve endings, which can be found at the top of your vulva. It is protected by a delicate flap of skin that varies in shape and size. This flap of skin is called the clitoral hood.

If your clitoris is not apparent immediately or if you are not able to find that tiny nub at the top of the vulva, you can try coaxing it out by touching or stroking the area gently, or better still, ask your partner to lick the top of your vulva to stimulate your clitoris.

Once you feel aroused, the clitoris will become engorged and protrude slightly. And then, it will be easier for you to spot it. If your partner is groping around in the dark to find your clitoris, tell him what feels good and when you start feeling aroused, or better yet, just guide his fingers towards that hot spot.

Now that you know how to find the clitoris, try out this step-by-step guide to achieving super orgasms.

A Step-By-Step Guide To Super Orgasms

- Continue stimulating your clitoris by gently stroking it. You will start feeling a wave-like sensation, with your legs and pelvis grooving in with the flow. You can also ask your partner to lick the part and you are sure to start groaning with pleasure as he licks more and more, creating waves of super pleasure for you.

- Try using a sex toy or a vibrator and insert it just beneath the clitoral hood until its soft gel tip touches or is pressed against your G-spot. It is the spongy area located at the front wall of your vagina, just behind the urethra. You can play around this region until it feels right.

- Now, contract your vaginal and pelvic muscles rhythmically around the vibrating toy as you move it against the G-spot while your partner licks your clitoris.

- Continue massaging your clitoris (or let your partner do it for you) until you feel close to orgasm.

- Do not stop even when you feel the orgasm building. Keep the toy in place while you are coming. It is natural to want to pull the toy away or stop stimulating the clitoris further, but pulling away might prevent the super orgasm from occurring.

- For best results, ask him to run his tongue over the sides of the clitoris and the clitoral hood.

- Keep stroking your clitoris until you are getting those waves of pleasure. You can go on and on enjoying one orgasm after another. The idea is to not to stop until you know you have got a super orgasm.

It's only you who can define what a super orgasm means to you or how many times you must get an orgasm to call it a super orgasm. So, keep stimulating, and enjoy the pleasure and the power to get as many orgasms as you want or you can, until you know it's a super orgasm!

Remember one thing, the vagina is an incredible thing. The more you experiment with it, the more you will learn about what you can do with it and what it can do for you!

If you would like to add some more fun to your orgasms, you can try different positions. Let me share with you the best sex positions that you can try to get orgasms and super orgasms.

Four Best Sexual Positions To Get Orgasms

Free-As-Air Position

In this position, your man lies down on his back and you sit down on his penis, facing the other way. Then, taking your own time, you lower yourself gradually such that your back is lying outstretched on the front of his body while still having his penis inside you.

You will feel genuinely free-as-air or weightless, which is quite a novel sensation. Your partner can touch, caress, and stimulate your clitoris more easily in this position. So it's going to be different and fun with much more stimulation and more orgasms.

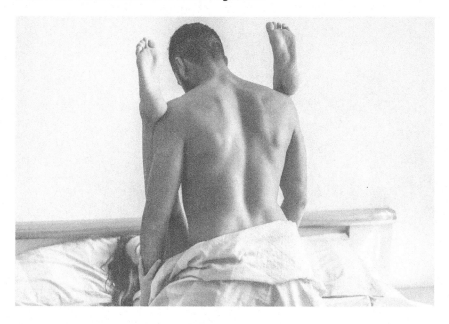

The CAT Position

The term CAT here stands for the 'coital adjusted technique'. However, you don't have to let these rather boring and technical terms put you off!

Essentially, it is a face-to-face position with your man riding much higher than he would in the missionary position, such that his shoulders and head are at least six inches higher up from the bed than usual.

What this means is that his penis would not go all the way into your vagina. Instead, the root or stem of the penis will only be pulled hard against your clitoris – producing those great sensations in that little all-important organ of yours.

You can try this position to get those super orgasms right for you. Some couples do this with the man's legs outside, though you can also try it with his legs inside yours. Some couples find that they cannot thrust much deeper with this position. So, this kind of makes them 'rock' together!

The CAT position certainly produces a very different sensation from most other sexual positions. It's definitely worth a try. It might just take you to the new heights of ecstasy every time you get into it.

Pinner Position

To try this position, lie flat on your front and ask your man to lie face down on top of you. He then penetrates you from behind. Since you are lying flat on the bed, you will get completely different sensations from those from-behind positions where your bottom is up in the air.

You can also slip your hand in between your body and the bed and rub your clitoris to intensify the pleasure further.

Women who usually do not come during intercourse are often able to experience climax and orgasm in this position.

The Spoons Position

In this position, you lie on your side while your partner lies behind you, curled around your bottom (like the spoons in a drawer), and then enters you from behind. The great advantage of this position is that both of you can reach down to rub your clitoris. What's even better is that neither of you has to take the weight of the other.

So, it could be a good position if you are missing out on great orgasms and can't enjoy sex much due to joint pains or other health issues. Believe me; there's no one right or wrong way to enjoy sex and get orgasms. All couples have to experiment to find what works for them.

Yes, I am sure that trying out different positions will add great fun and excitement to this already pleasurable activity and help you have a long super orgasmic experience!

Chapter 12
Reaching The Core Of Orgasms

What works for one woman could be uncomfortable for another. So, basically, you need to try out different ways to arouse yourself and try out different tricks to get yourself to come.

Let me share with you some tips to try out while having self-orgasms or having sex with your partner to create a sensual space where orgasms (and arousal) ebb and flow.

More Foreplay

Enough has already been said about the importance of foreplay. Fantasy, expectation, and anticipation are all parts of the process of getting there. So, let me emphasise once more that you have to take your time with foreplay. A long foreplay can get you in the mood and ensure you are connected at a different level. It can also lead to maximum arousal for you and your partner.

Start With A Kiss!

Kissing will reduce the secretion of a stress hormone called cortisol, and in turn, quicken the time that you and your partner will need to feel turned on. Tilt your head to the right while you pay lip service.

This makes you appear more caring, flooding you and your partner's systems with the 'connection' hormone oxytocin, thus building trust and encouraging both of you to feel closer and relaxed.

Nibble At The Neck

After a few moments of passionate kissing, move your lips down to your partner's neck. You can also slide off the lips to his or her neck occasionally while kissing for sensual arousal.

Undress

The most effective way to get aroused is not to undress yourself but to let your partner do it for you. Each time you go in for a peck or a kiss, remove an item of your partner's clothing too. Getting naked shows enthusiasm! The sight of your partner's naked body will surely boost your desire to get more intimate.

Touch and caress each part of your partner's body as you undress each other. If you feel good when you are naked, you are more likely to climax.

Use Lube

Once your vulva is stimulated or aroused, it will produce a natural lubricant. But in case the juices are not flowing, apply a small quantity of lubricant.

You can try different vaginal lubricants as discussed earlier. There are many types available in different fragrances. You can ask your partner to squeeze a few pumps of the lubricant onto his fingers and slip them into your knickers. Spread the lubricant close to the vaginal opening and continue with stimulating the clitoris with the same fingers for further arousal.

Be Vocal

The key to getting good orgasms might actually come from talking about sex. Normalising talking about sex can help you create a comfortable space in your relationship, and help you verbalise what you want at 'that' moment. So, make sure you do not limit your sex talks to the bedroom.

You can chat outside of your bedroom, discuss and plan different ways to enjoy sex, talk about how it feels to get closer, and so on. When you allow yourself to be vocal about sex and self-pleasure, you also allow more blood to flow into your pelvic floor, vaginal canal, cervix, and most importantly, your clitoris.

This will make it easier for you to feel aroused and stimulated, to have great sex and get great orgasms.

Explore Multimedia

Watch or read some sexy stuff like erotica or listen to some hot music to get your senses aroused for those intimate moments. You can also fantasise while you watch or read that sexy stuff, imagining yourself to be in that position.

What you need right now is just a small push to get yourself to reach there. You have almost reached an orgasm. You know what to do, and how to do it. You just need to put these tricks into practice and try out different positions and experiment with your sex life. This is all you need to do to get those super orgasms. And once you get your first one, I am sure you will not be able to stop smiling!!!

Chapter 13
Diving Deeper Into Foreplay
To Improve Your Orgasms

Whether you have been in a relationship recently or for a long time, you know what foreplay can do to your orgasms. And you do not even have to be in a relationship to understand the pleasure foreplay can bring. Young women who have never got closer to a man also get that feeling when they imagine their breasts caressed or their nipples pinched.

If you don't believe it, you can try doing it to yourself, now. Just hold your breasts with both your hands and squeeze them gently. Lie down naked and pinch or fondle your nipples. You will realise your breath is getting faster and your thighs are pressing together. That's just a glimpse of what foreplay can do to you. Does it end there? No... foreplay has much more to offer than just playing with your breasts and nipples. Let's dive deeper into foreplay and check out some amazing tricks that will help you get super orgasms.

10 Ways To Spice Up Your Sex Life And Get Super Orgasms With Foreplay

Indulge In Fantasising

Spontaneity and imagination can create excitement that will build you up toward great orgasms. When and how you want to start building it up is up to you. It can be a few minutes before you want to get intimate or even several hours earlier, when both of you are distant, apart at your workplaces or homes.

Just imagining what you will do when you meet up will let you enjoy 'no holds barred' sex. Imagine yourself hugging each other closely with your arms around his neck and then crashing on the bed with the anticipation of him loving and fondling all parts of your body. You don't have to settle for what worked earlier. Simply imagine what makes you feel aroused. You can also send him erotic messages to give him a hint of what you want and how you want him to cross all boundaries of erotica when you meet. Keep building it up so that you can't wait to even get to the bedroom. You know you are going to have great sex when your man holds you tight and starts to get very very intimate with you, fondling you all over your breasts, thighs, and neck, passionately pushing you against the wall, or the sofa, or the chair, or the bed!

Whisper Into His Ear

Some dirty talk whispered into his ear can give him a clue that you want more. After all; who whispers when there is no one around?! Whispering into his ear, telling him how much you are enjoying what he is doing and how you don't want him to hold back, will encourage him to get wilder with his kissing, boob pressing, and nipple fondling.

Passionate Kiss

Kissing is a classic part of foreplay. Remember the first time you kissed someone? If you do, you already know that kisses are the ultimate test of your feelings for each other and one of the fastest ways to connect with your man. A simple yet intense and passionate kiss as he presses your entire body against his can arouse your senses and help you get closer and closer to getting super orgasms.

Allow yourself to feel the full-body contact, with his body brushing against yours, while paying attention to the textures, pressure, and contours of your bodies. Touch every inch of each other's body to promote full-body orgasms. Start at the head, work your way down the back of the body, and change the pressure, strokes, and movement across the entire surface of the skin to realise all your sexual fantasies.

Awaken Your Senses

Now is the time to create some suspense by taking the foreplay a step further with a sensual game. Blindfold your partner to heighten his other senses. Then, touch your nipples, fingers, lips, or tongue on different parts of his body, and ask him to guess the body part.

Use Your Mouth On Him

Ask him to lick you in your sensitive spots like your nipples, clitoris, and G-spot. Gesture him to come closer to you with an all-knowing smile. Hover your mouth very close to his mouth to build anticipation. And then, tease him by pulling away when you get close enough for a kiss.

This will surely make your man go wilder. He will then definitely go down for your breasts and work his way around your now-erect nipples. Yes, by this time, your nipples would be stimulated, making them more pointed. At this moment, just a touch of his lips to your nipples will make you go oh... and ahhh... You will notice your thighs rising up and getting restless for more and more action. Ask him to pinch your nipples and bite them. With every bite, you will feel aroused.

Playing With Nipples

Ask him to keep biting your nipple while he squeezes your other breast with his hands. You can also bring both your breasts closer so that he can bite both the nipples together. Wow! This is something you will surely love. The thing is your boobs are bound to slip out from his teeth when he tries to bite both your nipples together. And this 'pulling away' sensation will give you pain that will heighten your orgasms to a new level! Now, get on the top and hold both your breasts in your hands and bring them closer to him to let him bite them. Just as he tries to rise to bite them, move away. Do this a few times to get him to want to have them. Within no time, he will pull you closer and hold you tightly so that, this time, you can not move away and he gets to bite your nipples. Try pulling away slightly at this point and you will feel orgasmic pleasure running all over you

Don't Ignore The Other Parts

Get to know each other's bodies like the backs of your hands. You can amp up the anticipation by using the backs of your hands to build arousal. You do not have to grab, apply pressure, or knead right away. Instead, just use feather-light touch to caress the back of your partner. Ask him to give you a 'thigh job' using his fingers, tongue, palms, sex toys, and lips to kiss, slither, or lick all around your inner thighs without diving in between your legs. And don't forget 'the Pussy Pocket'. Guide your man's palm to your vagina and fold all his five fingers over your vulva.

He will take the hint and press his fingers against your vaginal lips to create heat. Ask him to rub slowly and gently, and then increase the pressure and pace by following the rhythm of your hips. Then, he can push his full hand against your vagina, or undulate in a wave-like fashion to stimulate your clitoris. This is one of the best foreplay methods that guarantee orgasms. If you wind up wanting more stimulation, use a vibrator for the act.

For most women, erotic foreplay is more exciting than the intercourse itself. From those sultry glances from across the room to sleazy make-out sessions, foreplay can spice up your sex life and allow you to explore sensations that will send waves of orgasms throughout your body. So, when you have some dirty plan up your sleeve, go all about it and let nothing come between you and orgasms!

Chapter 14
The Best Sex Toys For Passionate Sex

Sex toys are designed to give you more pleasure so that you can get better orgasms. And this is a great thing, especially because you can use it while having sex with your partner or even while masturbating. If there is any area of your body that you love to be stimulated, there will be a special sex toy available to do just that!

Choosing your sex toy comes down to which part of your body you want to target. Contrary to what most women believe, it's not limited to just the clitoris and vagina. Clitoris and vagina are definitely the two most popular body parts that female sex toys target. But there are all sorts of other sex toys for you to try.

Here's a quick sex toy guide that will give you an idea of how you can choose your sex toy for all different kinds of orgasms and sexual pleasures.

Dildo

It is the most popular sex toy for women. Much of its popularity comes from its versatility. Dildos are non-vibrating sex toys that you can use for internal massage and penetration. They usually have an anatomical design, which looks like a replica of a penis. You can try a mini dildo, a big dildo, a glass or metal dildo, or a curved dildo that targets the G-spot directly.

Vibrators

The buzz in your bedroom would probably be incomplete without a vibrator. Well... that's because these toys are designed with the intention of helping women achieve super orgasms, no matter which part of the body you use them on.

You can use a vibrator as an all-encompassing sex toy to stimulate all the erogenous zones of your body. Figure out which could be the best vibrator for you based on the areas of your body you would like to have stimulated, like your vagina, G-spot, clitoris, or nipples.

Clitoral Massager

It is one of the best female sex toys for clitoral stimulation. Use it to achieve heightened sexual stimulation and get super orgasms. You will find all sorts of clitoral massagers available for you, from the powerful, large wand vibrators to the smaller bullet vibrators. You can use the bullets alone or with your partner during sex. They are so small they won't get in your way.

Nipple Clamps

Your nipples are one of the erogenous zones of your body and yet they are often overlooked by sex toy users. Nipple clamps are usually associated with pain, which itself brings pleasure. Choosing the right nipple clamp that pinches your nipples can beat all other kinds of sexual stimulation. When tugged on, these clamps do cause some pain. But the main purpose of these clamps is actually the effect that comes when they are removed. Once you remove the clamps, you will experience a rush of sensations that make your nipples more sensitive and responsive to pinching, touching, biting, and licking.

Electric Toothbrush

If you feel too shy to buy a sex toy, you can still use some common household things to convert them into your own sex toys. For example; your electric toothbrush can double up as your sex toy, thanks to its vibration capabilities. You just have to press the vibrating handle of your toothbrush against the area between your labia to stimulate your vagina and clitoris.

Foods

Yes, some fruits and vegetables like cucumber, carrot, zucchini, banana, and Japanese eggplants are great choices as your readily-available sex toys. You can roll a medium-sized fruit like a plum or a tomato in a circular motion over your clitoris for some stimulation.

Ice Cubes

Ice cubes are great to tantalise or tease your partner. Slowly run a cube over your nipples during foreplay and then slide it down your torso, and see how long he can withstand not getting intimate with you.

Hairbrush

A hairbrush can be good for penetration. The rubber handle of the hairbrush can be great to use with your partner or on yourself. Make sure you put a condom over it to avoid infection, and use plenty of lubricants.

Spoon

You can use even a tablespoon for sexual stimulation. Just place its rounded bottom part on your clitoris. Then, rub it out in a slow circular motion.

What's great about the spoons is they do not have sharp edges and they are super-smooth against the skin.

Cellphone

You can turn your cellphone into a vibrator by simply downloading a vibration app. Most of these apps have the option to change the intensity levels for you to play around with. Use it over clothing or put your vibrating phone in a sock instead of using it directly on your skin in order to prevent infection.

Whichever sex toys you are using, make sure you follow proper hygienic practices and avoid using them for any other purposes later in order to protect yourself against infections.

Chapter 15
Best Essential Oils For Erotic Stimulation And Super Orgasms

Aromatherapy using essential oils can create a mood that can enhance your orgasms several notches higher. These aromatherapy oils work in different ways and need to be used in different manners to increase your arousal.

Here are some of the best aromatherapy oils you can use to get your intimate moments to click like never before.

Lavender

Lavender oil is the best when it comes to increasing your orgasmic pleasure. You can add lavender essential oil to a diffuser, and let its aroma fill your bedroom or living room a few minutes before he arrives. The fresh and erotic scent of lavender will give him an idea of your plans to get super-naughty, and in no time you will be on the couch kissing and fondling.

Rose Oil

How about applying rose oil on your skin to entice your man to get closer and do all that is required to make your sexual fantasies come true? Rose oil is readily absorbed through the skin. Once absorbed, it stays in the applied part and makes you smell sensuous and erotic.

You can also ask your man to use this oil to massage your body. As he moves his hands all over your body during the massage, you will feel every part getting aroused for an intense sexual act.

Ylang Ylang

Have you ever dreamt of entering the bath with your man? This thought itself is so titillating! Add a few drops of ylang ylang oil to your warm bubble bath, and a few drops to your bedroom diffuser. The results are incredible!

Ylang ylang will stimulate your senses by acting as a natural aphrodisiac and enhance your desire to get more and more intimate. After the bath, he will definitely be carrying you naked back to the bed for some more action and great sex.

Clary Sage

Add a few drops of clary sage essential oil in the diffuser or simply spray it in your room when you want to enjoy sex the whole night with no 'terms and conditions'! Clary sage is a powerful natural aphrodisiac that will keep up your sense of arousal all night long and allow you to make love again and again.

Sandalwood Oil

Spray sandalwood oil or apply it on your skin to enhance the feeling of wanting more sex. It is so soothing and relaxing that both of you will forget all your worries and look only to get as intimate as possible. These essential oils will find a permanent place in your bedroom once you have tested how they perk up your sexual pleasure.

Try different essential oils in different ways to get a new kind of sexual pleasure every time. The benefits are endless! You will see yourself bringing your sexual fantasies into reality by getting better with each orgasm!

Summary

Sexual intercourse's common dilemma? Painful sex. If we are being real, none of us can deny how amazing having sexual intercourse with our loved ones is, but it could become even more amazing if we can achieve orgasm without feeling any pain from doing it. There are many reasons why painful sex occurs, and it is something not to be ashamed of as there are valid reasons behind it. One important reason is trauma a woman experienced in the past. It could also be due to surgery or an accident that led to the swelling of the woman's genital region, increasing the risk of pain during sex; trauma due to sexual abuse; or infection and inflammation of the genital area.

Another factor that causes painful sexual intercourse is a woman's mental health. Insecurities about physical appearance have added to women's worries, shifting their focus from having an orgasm to being conscious of how they look while being intimate with their partner. With this, momentum is lost, decreasing vaginal lubrication and leading to painful penetration. The causes of pain during sex don't just stem from the reasons mentioned above. Another possible reason could be the age of the woman. She might be menopausal, causing natural lubrication to decrease and making her partner's entrance a little bit painful. So, to summarise the possible reasons, painful sex may have been caused by two different factors: pain by penetration, and/or pain caused by emotional factors.

However, despite all the valid reasons stated above, and even though we are transitioning to a more open society where sex education is being incorporated into educational curricula, for example, some women still find consulting professionals about painful sex to feel a little bit shameful. Let's admit it, even if many people are becoming more accepting of this kind of topic, there are still a lot who seem to find discussing such conditions a little scandalous — making some other women who are experiencing painful sex hesitant to open up about their situation. Still, we should not stop encouraging women who suffer from this condition to come out and to not mind society's judgement about their sexual life.

In relation to this, suppressing painful sex can lead to many serious conditions that might damage a person's personal relationship with their partner and the people around them. Another concerning consequence of painful sex is the inability to get pregnant. Let's first discuss its effect on mental health and social relationships. It has been mentioned that one of the reasons why painful sex occurs is because of a woman's mental state. However, suppose painful intercourse isn't going to be treated; in that case, it may lead a woman's already unstable mental health to become even poorer than it already is or make a woman with healthy mental stability anxious, making her mental strength deteriorate.

An early sign that you are experiencing mental health consequences of painful sex is when you get easily stressed and anxious before, during, and after sexual intercourse – which may lead to short-term or long-term emotional damage. Another result of painful sex ignorance is depression. Women who suffer from this consequence of painful sex tend to experience abnormal behavior in terms of their personal interactions. They tend to become more aloof. They avoid conversations with their friends and even family to the point of completely isolating themselves, just because they want to avoid people who might ask about their personal lives.

On the other hand, late consultation of painful sex can make conception difficult, if not impossible. One, if the woman can't tolerate the pain of having intercourse, it will really be difficult to conceive. Two, as mentioned, infertility is also a potential result of disregarding the condition for a long time. Couples trying to conceive would just usually become aware of the effects of painful sex after consulting a doctor, which is often too late. It is important to note that painful sex is one of the early signs of infertility. For example, suppose uterine fibroids or endometriosis are the cause of discomfort during sex; these require treatment if they interfere with one's fertility.

That is why it is imperative for every woman experiencing pain during sex not to feel ashamed, as there is more to it than minding other people's judgement. While painful sexual intercourse sounds alarming, do not worry because there are many available remedies for it. With those remedies, achieving a mindblowing orgasm will no longer be impossible. First on the list is a much longer time spent on foreplay. Foreplay should be given much more attention because this is where the woman and her partner are building up the momentum. Couples need to set the mood of intimacy to feel aroused and to stimulate the woman's vulva or vagina.

The more the woman feels turned on, the more vaginal lubrication will be produced, making penetration smoother and decreasing the risk of painful sex. There are many ways to heighten arousal and sexual tension between couples looking to reach a climax. One way couples may try is the nibbling of the woman's nipples. Couples can try massaging the woman's breasts or nibble or play with her nipples as they are one of the erogenous zones of a woman's anatomy. The nerve endings in the nipples when nibbled or massaged produce sensations that can sustain an intimate momentum. Rubbing the woman's clitoris during foreplay may also help, as it is highly sensitive when touched or rubbed, which will be of great help in making the vulva more lubricated.

In contrast to this, if increasing vaginal lubrication through prolonged foreplay still doesn't work, then you may opt for using lubricant gels to reduce the friction causing painful penetration. Another remedy you can try is a change in position. Trying this out may just change your sexual intercourse experience for the better, as many couples have reported intercourse improvements when they tried exploring different positions. Explore as many positions as you can or as you want until you find the perfect position to reach the ultimate version of climax: super orgasm. In addition to this, following a certain step-by-step process to overcome painful intercourse is actually one of the best remedies you may also want to try.

A system you can use as reference is the Pain Free System. This system is a quick guide to the key actions that you should do on a regular basis to achieve the results you're looking for – a sexually fulfilling life. Here are the steps you should follow if you want to try the Pain Free System: Diagnosis, Options, Body Knowledge, Causes, and Solutions. You may also want to try doing an exercise that focuses on the muscles of the lower pelvic region, as the muscles located here have a big contribution to painful sex triggers. Here are some of the best exercises you can try to strengthen the muscles in this area: child pose, happy baby pose, diaphragmatic breathing, Kegel, and aerobic exercise.

Ensuring the strength of pelvic floor, abdominal and vaginal muscles will reduce the risk of painful intercourse. Another effective natural remedy to relieve painful sex is watching the food you eat. It is already well known that a sexually fulfilling life is also dependent on being physically and emotionally fit. Therefore, changing your diet could also help you overcome painful sex. You may want to include apple in your diet, as it can help in the stimulation of blood flow from the genitalia and vagina, causing sexual arousal – thanks to the antioxidants the fruit contains.

Another food that you should try is oysters. Just like apples, oysters help in the increase of blood flow which is necessary when building up an intimate mood.

Foods that help in blood flow stimulation are good to try if you want to achieve a better sexual life. Advanced treatments are also available if none of the aforementioned remedies work on your condition. With this, you may want to rely on the advancement of technologies that we have today. One example would be laser therapy. It provides wonderful treatments for excessive vaginal dryness and the slowing down of age-related vaginal atrophy by stimulating collagen and elastin production. This treatment also offers long-term solutions to women who suffer from a non-tolerable level of painful sexual intercourse, thus, preventing painful sex complications.

Once you have overcome the challenges of painful sex, there are different types of orgasms that both you and your partner can possibly reach: vaginal, cervical, nipple, G-spot, continuous, and super orgasm are just some of the types of orgasms you can experience depending on how you and your partner perform sexual intercourse. As mentioned above, you can try as many positions as you can or as you want! Reaching a mindblowing orgasm is not only dependent on all of the factors mentioned above, but also on how you make your sexual intercourse as steamy as possible. Finally, freeing yourself from suffering is what should always matter.

At the end of the day, painful sex isn't just going to affect your sexual life, but also your mental and physical health. People must learn that wanting to treat painful sex isn't just all about the human libido, as there are serious underlying concerns to painful sex when disregarded for a very long time. Having it treated is for the purpose of getting the life that women deserve – a mindblowing orgasm is just a bonus.

Acknowledgements

I give all the glory for this book to the Lord God Almighty who made it possible. I would also like to appreciate my darling wife for her support and suggestions, and for the peace of mind in my home. I must also thank all my children for their support.

I appreciate all members of my family, the 'Fash Family', especially for your prayers and encouragement that have kept me going. Thank you also to my support staff for their hard work and input. The contribution of my publisher has been tremendous. Her ideas and suggestions have enriched the book to a new level. I appreciate her and recommend her to anyone working on any kind of book.

Dedication

I dedicate this book to the Lord God Almighty who created man and woman and love, and who created sex for procreation and enjoyment, for His grace and mercy upon mankind who have oftentimes abused the privilege of sex.

I dedicate the book to every woman who has suffered the pain of sex in any form and has been deprived of the wonderful joy of sex.

Recommended Programmes & Seminars

How Would You Like To Be Able To ...
Have An Amazing Sexual Lifestyle?

I have prepared a special video guide to help you get your sex life to the desired level and beyond so that you can discover:
- a new approach to your sex life
- how to overcome painful intercourse
- how to eventually get a great orgasm
- healthy practices, exercises, and foods you can incorporate into your daily lifestyle

Purchase the **VIDEO GUIDE** here:
https://olufasogbon.podia.com/mind-blowing-orgasms-turn-pain-to-pleasure-video

Speaking Engagements
You can book me for keynote speaking engagements, for content speaking or for presentations regarding **Mindblowing Orgasms** at olu@olufasogbon.com

Strategic Alliances
If you have a business proposal or joint venture idea to collaborate with me, please don't hesitate to email me at olu@olufasogbon.com

Social Media:

I would highly appreciate a review on Amazon.

Follow me on social media and let me know which techniques from this book have worked for you.

Follow me on LinkedIn: Olu Fasogbon
https://www.linkedin.com/in/olufasogbon/

Follow me on Facebook: Olu Fasogbon
https://www.facebook.com/olufasogbon/

Follow me on Instagram: @olufasogbon
https://www.instagram.com/olufasogbon/

Useful Products:

How Would You Like To Look Younger & More Beautiful?

What if you could feel more energised, sleep better and have reduced pain? If the answer is yes, Glutathione is for you.

What is *Glutathione?*
Glutathione is a powerful antioxidant which combats alcohol use, a diet high in processed foods, stress and trauma, chronic sickness, and other illnesses.

Some benefits:
- Boosts energy
- Strengthens the immune system of your body
- Lessens the harmful effects of stress
- Increases athletic efficiency and speed of recovery
- Reduces the ageing process
- Cleanses your cells and liver
- Enhances sleep quality
- Improves concentration and mental clarity
- Reduces pain in the muscles and joints
- Helps your skin glow

Get your SPECIAL OFFER NOW!
Simply click on the link below or scan the QR code:
https://olufasogbon.com/cellgevity/

Please Note:
Cellgevity is not a medication and we do not claim that it is used for the cure, treatment, mitigation, diagnosis or prevention of any medical condition or disease.

How Would You Like To Help Thousands Of People Improve Their Health & Benefit Financially As Well?

<u>Become A Max Associate</u>

Create a GLOBAL IMPACT that will change PEOPLE'S LIVES in terms of health and finances! Become a Max Associate. Promote health products and benefit from helping hundreds of people feel healthier, and improve your finances in the process.

Click on the link below or scan the QR code to join:
https://cellgevity.co.uk/join/

Would You Love To Lose Weight At Home?

Discover the only weight loss DVD you'll need to lose the weight desired so you can feel energised, have more fun and appreciate your body again, so you can fit into your 'skinny jeans' or the gorgeous dress at the back of your closet.

If you'd love to feel like YOU again – the way you used to be, when you loved your body – try this weight loss DVD and make your ex-boyfriend or ex-husband jealous he lost you.

Find the best video exercise that you can do in the comfort of your home! The routines in the video will surely help you lose weight quickly. The routines and the practices shown in this product are healthy ways of losing weight, and they could also help you boost your energy and improve your everyday mood.

Some Benefits:
1. You are going to have the best exercise DVD for weight loss.
2. Lose weight in the comfort of your own home.
3. Lose weight and feel better about yourself.
4. Be more active at home with our workout DVD course.
5. Get a slimmer waistline in just six weeks!
6. Lose weight without going to the gym.
7. Lose weight without dieting.
8. Be able to wear your favourite clothes again!

Ready to get fit? Order that video now by clicking on the link or scanning the QR code below:
https://weightlossathome.co.uk/product/weight-loss-at-home-dvd/

Would you like to have a **Complete Weight Loss Plan?**

Meta-Switch Weight Management Supplement Capsules are created as part of a healthy lifestyle. Making Meta-Switch part of your daily routine will help you with your weight management in a healthy manner – with no caffeine or other stimulants.

Meta-Switch is an innovative and unique weight loss system designed to:
1. Get you to your weight loss goals.
2. Switch on your metabolism and switch on healthy weight management!
3. Support a healthy metabolism.
4. Improve overall health and well-being.

START YOUR JOURNEY TO BETTER WEIGHT & HEALTH TODAY WITH META-SWITCH!

What's Your Weight Health?
Excess weight and fat can impair the immune system's ability to fight disease and puts you more at risk for certain diseases and debilitating conditions. Knowing your Weight Health can inform you about the potential risks you can face, giving you a big heads up about your overall health and wellness.

Join the thousands who are losing weight daily with the Meta-Switch Weight Loss Plan: https://cellgevity.co.uk/product/meta-switch/

TAKE ACTION TODAY & ORDER NOW:
USA - https://www.max.com/shop/index.php?id=DENUSA002002&categoryId=NDA=

UK - https://cellgevity.co.uk/product/meta-switch/

How Would You Like To Find A Safe Environment For Family Members Needing Supported Care and Accommodation?

Our supported care and accommodation centre offers 24-hour person-centred support to individuals with a learning disability, autism and/or delayed mental development identified through a health assessment, elderly, frail, Home Care Service and Live-in Care.

The aim of the service is to provide a safe and homely environment that promotes empowerment, independence, and choice, whilst enhancing the individual's daily living skills.

We are proud to be one of the leading providers of Supported Living and Home Care in the UK today.

Get this quality and family-like care by clicking on the link below or scanning the QR code:
https://supportedcareandaccommodation.org/

Want To Save Money On Your Gas And Electricity Bills & Be Eco-Friendly?

Discover a green energy solutions provider in the UK which can help you cut your bills at affordable prices
https://bestgasandelectricity.co.uk/

Some Benefits:
1. Reliable, with 24/7 Support
2. 100% Natural/Environmentally Friendly

Think Green. *Taking steps to be more eco-friendly can go a long way in saving the planet!*
This is the future. Be part of the global innovation.

1. Check our website **Plural Gas and Electricity** here:
 https://bestgasandelectricity.co.uk/
2. Get a quote by clicking on the box that says 'Get a Quote' on the upper-right part of your screen.
3. Fill out all the necessary information listed on the form. Don't forget to provide us with a message about your preferred date.
4. Wait for our call.

How Would You Like To Protect Your Home And Keep It Safe And Secure?

Discover our **Wireless Home Alarms** so you can have **peace of mind** at home and at work:
https://wirelesshomealarm.co.uk/

Plural Alarms strives to provide you with the greatest security solutions for your home and office. With our highly protective anti-burglar alarm systems, we secure and maintain your home security.

How You'll Benefit:
1. We offer advanced home security to keep you safe
2. We don't just provide the equipment, we also provide the guards to attend in the event of an intruder
3. Advanced 24/7 Alarm Receiving Centre
4. 24-hour Guard Response

Join millions that trust our services!
Check out the products and services we offer here or (scan QR code):
https://wirelesshomealarm.co.uk/

Resources (Photo Links):

[https://images.pexels.com/photos/568027/pexels-photo-568027.jpeg
auto=compress&cs=tinysrgb&dpr=1&w=500]

[https://www.yanhee.net/wp-content/uploads/female-perineum-anatomy.jpg]

[https://upload.wikimedia.org/wikipedia/commons/f/f9/1116_Muscle_of_the_Female_Perin
eum.png]

[https://images.pexels.com/photos/2947926/pexels-photo-2947926.jpeg?
auto=compress&cs=tinysrgb&dpr=1&w=500]

[https://images.pexels.com/photos/3724031/pexels-photo-3724031.jpeg?
auto=compress&cs=tinysrgb&dpr=1&w=500]

[https://images.pexels.com/photos/1510149/pexels-photo-1510149.jpeg?
auto=compress&cs=tinysrgb&dpr=1&w=500]

[https://images.pexels.com/photos/883441/pexels-photo-883441.jpeg?
auto=compress&cs=tinysrgb&dpr=1&w=500]

[https://images.pexels.com/photos/984949/pexels-photo-984949.jpeg?
auto=compress&cs=tinysrgb&dpr=1&w=500]

[https://images.pexels.com/photos/3850752/pexels-photo-3850752.jpeg?
auto=compress&cs=tinysrgb&dpr=1&w=500]

[https://images.pexels.com/photos/1683975/pexels-photo-1683975.jpeg
auto=compress&cs=tinysrgb&dpr=2&h=650&w=94]

[https://images.pexels.com/photos/313690/pexels-photo-313690.jpeg?
auto=compress&cs=tinysrgb&dpr=1&w=500]

[https://images.pexels.com/photos/556667/pexels-photo-556667.jpeg?
auto=compress&cs=tinysrgb&dpr=1&w=500]

[https://images.pexels.com/photos/3758833/pexels-photo-3758833.jpeg?
auto=compress&cs=tinysrgb&dpr=1&w=500]

[https://images.pexels.com/photos/4033152/pexels-photo-4033152.jpeg?
auto=compress&cs=tinysrgb&dpr=1&w=500]

[https://images.pexels.com/photos/888894/pexels-photo-888894.jpeg?
auto=compress&cs=tinysrgb&dpr=1&w=500]

[https://images.pexels.com/photos/192474/pexels-photo-192474.jpeg?
auto=compress&cs=tinysrgb&dpr=1&w=500]

[https://images.pexels.com/photos/4498316/pexels-photo-4498316.jpeg?
auto=compress&cs=tinysrgb&dpr=1&w=500]

[https://images.pexels.com/photos/4098374/pexels-photo-4098374.jpeg?
auto=compress&cs=tinysrgb&dpr=2&h=650&w=940]

[https://images.pexels.com/photos/163944/pexels-photo-163944.jpeg?
auto=compress&cs=tinysrgb&dpr=1&w=500]

[https://images.pexels.com/photos/3273989/pexels-photo-3273989.jpeg?
auto=compress&cs=tinysrgb&dpr=1&w=500]

[https://images.pexels.com/photos/2035066/pexels-photo-2035066.jpeg?
auto=compress&cs=tinysrgb&dpr=1&w=500]

[https://images.pexels.com/photos/3759657/pexels-photo-3759657.jpeg?
auto=compress&cs=tinysrgb&dpr=1&w=500]

[https://images.pexels.com/photos/1850629/pexels-photo-1850629.jpeg?
auto=compress&cs=tinysrgb&dpr=1&w=500]

[https://cdn.pixabay.com/photo/2017/07/06/09/36/jungle-gernnium-2477473__340.jpg]

[https://cdn.pixabay.com/photo/2017/03/26/21/54/yoga-2176668__340.jpg]

[https://cdn.pixabay.com/photo/2017/08/02/20/24/people-2573216__340.jpg]

[https://cdn.pixabay.com/photo/2017/07/28/13/29/spices-2548653__340.jpg]

[https://cdn.pixabay.com/photo/2018/01/06/18/40/relaxation-3065577__340.jpg]

[https://cdn.pixabay.com/photo/2015/12/09/17/11/vegetables-1085063__340.jpg]

[https://cdn.pixabay.com/photo/2018/03/21/23/21/nuts-3248743__340.jpg]

[https://cdn.pixabay.com/photo/2018/06/22/13/52/beetroot-3490809__340.jpg]

[https://static.toiimg.com/thumb/77996800.cms?
width=680&height=512&imgsize=1271494]

[https://cdn.pixabay.com/photo/2016/10/28/21/15/feet-1779064__340.jpg]

[https://nypost.com/wp-content/uploads/sites/2/2020/02/woman-orgasm-time-02.jpg?
quality=80&strip=all&w=1024]

[https://www.nydailynews.com/resizer/EEjNLHkNqvlHdxeG9xOXOeI1tNw=/415x276/top/ar
c-anglerfish-arc2-prod-
tronc.s3.amazonaws.com/public/Z26PANBLFSYFD5TYFKHR7TP7J4.jpg]

[https://cdn.crello.com/api/media/medium/397680346/stock-photo-cropped-view-man-
undressing-woman?token=]

[https://nypost.com/wp-content/uploads/sites/2/2020/02/woman-orgasm-time-02.jpg?
quality=80&strip=all&w=1024]

Other Books Recommended By Brand For Speakers Programme:

Speakers Are Leaders: Empower Yourself To Start Your Speaking Career

Lily Patrascu & Harry Sardinas

Peak Performance Sales: Turbocharge Your Sales Without Being Pushy

Lily Patrascu

Born To Stand Out, Not To Fit In: Empower Yourself To Live An Extraordinary Life

Teuta Avdyli

Reinvent Yourself: Discover The Brilliance Within & Create Infinite Possibilities

Adaobi Onyekweli

The Entrepreneur Paradox: The Easy Way To Achieve Balance & Wealth

Sandro Heitor

Dare To Be Imperfect: Stop Doubting Yourself And Go After What Your Want

Jimmy Asuni

Whatever It Takes: 5 Minutes A Day To Motivate Yourself & Achieve Your Goals

Victor Pabon

One Life, One List: The Ultimate Organization System To Create A Freedom Lifestyle

Christian Moser

Get Stuff Done: Productivity Hacks So You Can Do What You Love

Dee Lana

World-Changing Blockchain Opportunities: Generate Financial Freedom And Change The World With Blockchain, Bitcoin And Cryptocurrency

Sunny Ahonsi

Printed in Great Britain
by Amazon

19331336R00078